THE
FORCE
OF
JOY

FAITH A. OYEDEPO

The Force of Joy

Copyright © 2017 by:

Faith A. Oyedepo

ISBN 978--2480-36-3

Reprinted: 2018

Published in Nigeria by:
DOMINION PUBLISHING HOUSE

For further information or permission, address:
DOMINION PUBLISHING HOUSE
Km 10, Idiroko Road, Canaanland, Ota, Nigeria.
Tel: +234 816 406 0777, +234 909 151 4022

Or visit our website: ***www.dphprints.com***

Connect with Faith A. Oyedepo

 Faith Abiola Oyedepo   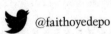 @faithoyedepo

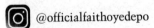 @officialfaithoyedepo   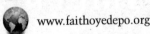 www.faithoyedepo.org

All Scripture quotations are from the King James Version of the Bible, except otherwise stated.

CONTENTS

Introduction

... That our joy may be full.

2 John 1:12

Joy is a major asset for fulfilment in life! If you must triumph at all times, the occurrences of life notwithstanding, you must learn to be joyful. In fact, a joyful person is an ever-winning person!

The truth is: You can handle anything when you are joyful! The life of Jesus Christ and other Bible characters attest to this fact. In contemporary life, we also see that joyful people are triumphant people!

In actual fact, to be joyless is to be helpless. This is because sorrow is an enemy to fulfilling destiny. Moreover, when you are downcast, you go down in life. The Bible says:

Heaviness in the heart of man maketh it stoop...

Proverbs 12:25

As Christians, maintaining a joyful life is the springboard of a praiseful life. This means that when joy is missing, there can be no songs of praise in your heart. If you are to be an ever praiseful saint, you must be a joyful saint! This is what makes joy essential in the life of a believer.

Even our service unto the Lord must be rendered with joy; otherwise, it will not be acceptable as seen in Deuteronomy 28:47-48:

> *Because thou servedst not the LORD thy God with joyfulness, and with gladness of heart... thou shalt serve thine enemies...*

You must maintain a heart that is full of joy as a matter of personal responsibility, if you must enjoy continuous triumph.

> *Speaking to yourselves in psalms and hymns and spiritual songs, singing and making melody in your heart to the Lord.*
>
> *Ephesians 5:19*

This book is written to empower you as a believer for a life of ceaseless triumph by being a joyful person! You will encounter an understanding of what true joy is and how it is different from just being happy. You will also see that a life of joy is a life of blessings. Joy has a source from which it can be drawn, for you to continuously experience it.

In addition, there are habits to be cultivated and things to be avoided at all cost, if joy must become your lifestyle!

Also, you will contact the Spirit of Joy, the driving force for a joyful life, which makes life to be enjoyed and not to be endured. Life is meant to be a blessing and not a burden, and the Spirit of Joy can make you a beneficiary of such!

Joy unspeakable is a reality and can be experienced by anyone who desires it. You can become a truly joyful person today, and those days of sorrow and mourning will be over! You will also enter into realms of ceaseless triumph, which is the heritage of the joyful!

Now sit back, read, understand the truths in this book and apply them. You will be glad you did!

Welcome to a life of ceaseless triumph!

1

What Is Joy?

...in thy presence is fulness of joy...

Psalm 16:11

Looking unto Jesus the author and finisher of our faith; who for the joy that was set before him endured the cross, despising the shame, and is set down at the right hand of the throne of God.

Hebrews 12:2

Joy is the product of a true relationship with God which cannot be faked or created by any human effort, otherwise, it will amount to mockery.

According to the *Webster's Dictionary*, joy means "a very glad feeling; happiness; great pleasure; delight."

Joy is also defined by the *American Dictionary of English Language* as "a shout; a proclamation that can manifest in singing; a triumph."

Both definitions give an idea of the meaning of joy, but they only define joy as the expression of an emotion. They fail to consider that joy is not just an expression of emotions; rather, it is a spiritual virtue. Therefore, to understand and experience the true meaning of joy, you will require a discovery of the source, the circumstances in which it is expressed and its attributes of longevity. In other words, the aforementioned must be considered before one can grasp the meaning of true joy.

The word "joy" appears severally in the Scripture: 88 times in 22 books of the Old Testament and 57 times in 18 books of the New Testament. These show the importance of joy. Besides, they give a comprehensive presentation of what God designed joy to be and represent in the life of a believer.

Joy is an essential spiritual virtue required for ceaseless triumphs in your journey to fulfilment of destiny. Therefore, if you don't want your destiny to wither, don't let your joy wither.

Just like grace, gratitude, love, hope and faith, joy is a much needed virtue. As air is needed to live, so joy is needed for a triumphant Christian life.

Joy is a force that oozes from your spirit man. It is a product of true relationship with God and cannot be formulated or created by human effort. An acronym can be derived from this three-letter word:

J stands for Jesus

O stands for Others

Y stands for Yourself

If life is taken in this order, true joy will never be lacking.

Joy and Happiness Compared

Joy, as a fruit of the Spirit, is from your spirit man. It is not in things, it is in you. This means that it cannot be affected by circumstances. Many people, however, mistake joy for happiness; but they are different, although inter-related. Joy is far deeper than happiness.

The truth is: You cannot be joyful without being happy, but you can be happy without being joyful.

Joy is a spiritual force referred to as the fruit of the Spirit, but happiness is a natural force

But the fruit of the Spirit is ... joy ...

Galatians 5:22

Since joy is a force of the Spirit, it means that it is a product of a regenerated spirit. New birth, therefore, becomes essential to experiencing the kind of joy referred to in this book.

In addition to new birth, a person must be filled with the Holy Spirit, in order to experience joy continually. This is because the Holy Spirit is the Spirit of Joy, and it is only an encounter with Him that keeps you fired up with joy in your spirit always.

Obviously, joy is neither a state of mind nor a passing sensation. It is a compelling spiritual force that, once allowed to reside in your heart, even the devil can't stand against it.

As a force of the Spirit, joy is a product of your encounter with the Word of God. This is because when we read and meditate on God's Word, it becomes a stimulant that stirs our spirit man.

Thy words were found, and I did eat them; and thy word was unto me the joy and rejoicing of mine heart...

Jeremiah 15:16

This is what makes it operate from within an individual's spirit or inner man.

On the other hand, happiness is an emotion that is subject to the happenings or circumstances around you; it is a function of your environment. In other words, joy is "within" but happiness is "around" or "outside".

Joy, therefore, is an internal, conscious belief, while happiness is a short-lived external emotion. Happiness, for instance, is the feeling you get when you buy something you desire, but joy goes beyond material things and feelings. This is why joy brings a feeling of contentment in life's storms, while happiness does not.

Joy is based on the Lord, while happiness is based on circumstances

A wise man once said, "Happiness depends on happenings; joy depends on Christ."

If joy, then, depends on Christ, we can again deduce that only those who have made Jesus Christ the Lord of their lives can encounter joy in the true sense of it.

Joy, according to Angela Thomas, is the inner attitude of rejoicing in one's salvation, regardless of outward circumstances. It is one of the fruits of a right relationship with God. This is why joy is said to be scarce, while happiness is everywhere. Joy is long-lasting, while happiness is temporary.

The good news is: You can receive Jesus Christ into your heart and life now; this act will bring joy along with it. Someone was quoted to have said, "For a long time, it seemed to me that life was about to begin – real life. But there was always some obstacle in the way, something to be gotten through first. Unfinished business ...then life will begin..." I will liken this unfinished business to the decision to make Christ the Lord of your life.

If you have not made Jesus Christ the Lord of your life and you desire to do so, please pray this prayer with me:

Heavenly Father, I come to You in the name of Jesus Christ. I admit that I am a sinner. Right now, I come to You and ask that You forgive me of my sins. Take control of my life; I give it all to You.

Your Word says that if I confess with my mouth that "Jesus is Lord," and believe in my heart that He died and resurrected on the third day, I will be saved (Romans 10:9).

I receive Your Word, therefore, I believe with my heart and I confess with my mouth that Jesus is the Lord and Saviour of my life. Help me to live every day in a way that pleases You. Write my name in the Lamb's Book of Life.

Thank You for saving me, in Jesus' name I pray. Amen.

Congratulations! You are now born again and have become a member of the family of God. Therefore, joy unspeakable full of glory becomes yours in Jesus' name.

Scriptural Examples of Joyful People

All through the Scripture, we see many examples of the effect of joy that flows from within. For instance, father Abraham had a promise from God that seemed to be delayed, but joy eventually brought about the fulfilment of that promise. The Bible records that:

He staggered not at the promise of God ... but was... giving glory to God; And being fully persuaded that, what he had promised, he was able...to perform.

Romans 4:20-21

15

Does a promise of God in your life seem delayed? Be joyful and there will be a speedy performance of that promise. In one of our Shiloh meetings in Nigeria, there was a couple who expected the fruit of the womb for many years. It looked as if the promise was delayed, but they held on to God's Word. When God rewarded their waiting, in fulfilment of the promise, He blessed them with quadruplets! God fast-forwarded their blessings! He can repeat the same in your own life!

Joseph, another example, was sold as a slave by his brothers to foreigners. In that foreign land, he ended up in a prison and it looked like the promise of being a ruler would never come to pass. However, this joyful Joseph ended up as Prime Minister, the second-in-command, to Pharaoh.

Joseph was a joyful person. This was why he could ask others why they were sad. As it is written:

> *And Joseph came in unto them in the morning, and looked upon them, and, behold, they were sad.*
>
> *And he asked...*
>
> *Wherefore look ye so sadly today...*
>
> Genesis 40:6-8

This attribute helped Joseph to end up on the throne. Though the road was full of thorns, yet, God gave him victory and he obtained the promise.

Thou shalt be over my house, and ...all my people ... only in the throne will I be greater than thou. And Pharaoh said unto Joseph, See, I have set thee over all the land of Egypt ...And Pharaoh said unto Joseph... without thee shall no man lift up his hand or foot in all the land of Egypt.

Genesis 41:40-44

Apostle Paul is another example of a joyful person in the Scripture. Not even prison could stop him from being joyful and singing praises to God.

...At midnight Paul and Silas prayed, and sang praises unto God... And suddenly there was a great earthquake ...and immediately all the doors were opened, and every one's bands were loosed.

Acts 16:25-26

What about David, the sweet psalmist? He fought so many battles, yet he lost none! As a joyful person, he always expressed gratitude joyfully to God, for who He was to him. As a result, God fought all his battles on his behalf, and gave him the victory!

Joy produced uncommon confidence in all these men. When you encounter this kind of joy, no matter the situation you may be confronted with, you are confident about life and the future. This is why it is called joy unspeakable, full of glory.

...yet believing, ye rejoice with joy unspeakable and full of glory.

1 Peter 1:8

This kind of joy, as mentioned earlier, oozes out of your being, even when there is no reason to be joyful. I believe this must be the reason the man of God, Robert Schuller, said, "Joy is not the absence of suffering; it is the presence of God!"

Joy is the "lubricant of life"; no matter what happens, when you are joyful, you enjoy life. Remember, life is meant to be enjoyed, and not to be endured!

Characteristics of Joyful People

Joyful people exhibit certain characteristics that make them unique and perpetually victorious. Let us consider some of these characteristics:

Joyful People Think Differently

Joyful people focus their thoughts on triumphs, rather than trials! In other words, they are not overwhelmed by the happenings around them, and as such have the ability to see what is ahead. This is what makes them "prisoners of hope" (Zechariah 9:12). They are visionaries, always seeing the positive side of every situation. My husband, Dr David Oyedepo, once said, "If you can see where you are going, you will not mind what is happening."

Joyful people are hopeful people; they eventually emerge triumphant in life, no matter the circumstance. Indeed, *For as he thinketh in his heart, so is he...* (Proverbs 23:7).

This way of thinking is not a common trait to many people, but evident in joyful people.

Joyful People Talk Differently

Their thoughts eventually reflect in their speech.

> *...out of the abundance of the heart the mouth speaketh.*
>
> Matthew 12:34

The result of thinking differently is talking differently! When you hear a joyful man speak, especially in the midst of adverse circumstances of life, you will wonder if he is in touch with reality. The truth is that they are well aware of what is happening, but they have some other truths from the Word of God that give them confidence and assurance that all will be well.

The Scripture says:

> *For verily I say unto you, That whosoever shall say unto this mountain, Be thou removed, and be thou cast into the sea; and shall not doubt in his heart, but shall believe that those things which he saith shall come to pass; he shall have whatsoever he saith.*

Mark 11:23

The questions are: Why will you keep magnifying what you do not want, when you have a better report that tells you what you desire? Why will you despise what God has to offer and continue to hold on to adverse circumstances, rather than what God has promised in His Word? Joyful people talk about victory rather than defeat! You, too, can start speaking victory, rather than defeat, and you will soon begin to experience it.

Joyful People Act Differently

Joyful people think and talk differently, and this is why they act differently. Show me a joyful man and I will show you a triumphant man in the making!

It is the attribute of joyfulness in their lives that makes them act differently. This virtue is prominent in the life of God's servant, Dr David Oyedepo. It makes him defy all the odds and take giant steps in the pursuit of his dreams and fulfilment of God's calling upon his life.

Clearly, joyful people always demonstrate a different attitude and disposition to adverse circumstances and situations in life; this is why they live a life of ceaseless triumph!

"Joy is an essential spiritual virtue that empowers for a life of ceaseless triumph."

- Faith A. Oyedepo

2
Fundamentals Of Joy

And the angel said unto them, Fear not: for, behold,
I bring you good tidings of great joy, which shall be
to all people.

For unto you is born this day in the city of David a
Saviour, which is Christ the Lord.

Luke 2:10-11

The birth of Jesus Christ brought joy into the world. This is very notable because it signifies God's goodwill towards man, as it shows that His plan is for us to be joyful. This implies that there is no reason to be downcast, no matter your present situation.

Therefore, it is very important to understand some

of the fundamentals of joy, if we are to fully experience it.

Joy is a Commandment

God commands us to be joyful.

Rejoice in the Lord alway: and again I say, Rejoice.

Philippians 4:4

I cannot overstate the fact that you are to remain joyful, especially if you desire God's intervention in negative circumstances. God commanded us to be ever joyful, and He will not ask us to do what is beyond our ability to obey.

For this is the love of God, that we keep his commandments: and his commandments are not grievous.

1 John 5:3

When you obey God's commandment, He makes you a commander of circumstances and situations.

Habakkuk 3:18-19 says:

Yet I will rejoice in the LORD, I will joy in the God of my salvation. The LORD God is my strength, and he will make my feet like hinds' feet, and he will make me to walk upon mine high places.

Joy is a Choice and not a Gift

The Bible does not refer to joy as a gift, but a fruit of the Spirit.

... the fruit of the Spirit is ... joy ...

Galatians 5:22

As a fruit, the demand is that you make a choice to be joyful and deliberately pursue it. This is because both sorrow and joy are choices; however, wise men choose joy.

Remember, happiness is temporary but joy is permanent. Very few people are joyful, while so many are happy because of the circumstances in which they find themselves. When their circumstances change, their happiness disappears.

The truth is: Happiness is easy to come by, but joy is very scarce. The good news is that, the scarce commodity of joy shall become a common commodity in your life from now on!

Joy is not automatic! It is a choice you must make, not just for today, but every day of your life. Therefore, deliberately choose joy!

Joy can be likened to a candle; until you light it, you can never enjoy it! Do not be bothered about what is happening, rather look forward to the greater and better things that are about to happen in your life.

Why Should We Choose Joy?

The Bible clearly commands us to choose joy.

It is written:

Rejoice evermore.

1 Thessalonians 5:16

Joy is a commandment from generation to generation.

Finally, my brethren, rejoice in the Lord. To write the same things to you ...is safe. -

Philippians 3:1

Our joy is for God's glory. When we radiate joy, God is glorified.

To appoint unto them ...the oil of joy ...that he might be glorified.

Isaiah 61:3

Joy is a choice that transforms lives. Most of us know how to enjoy God's gifts, but the pursuit of joy actually transforms us. However, the power to choose joy comes by the help of the Holy Spirit.

Joy has the mission to keep us focused on God.

Joy is not self-centred; therefore, pursuing joy and glorifying God are not in conflict. To pursue joy with your whole life is to honour the One, Who has given you life. God is glorified when we find our joy, peace and purpose in Him. Therefore, we must fight to retain our joy and our relationship with God.

The natural tendency is to be downcast, when things are not working the way we expect. However, being miserable does not solve the problem; joy actually does. This is because if the devil cannot steal your joy, he cannot steal your goods.

Therefore, the mission of joy in our lives is to keep us focused on God, until our desired change takes place. This is why distractions to our joy must be fought, as well as whatever wants to steal our joy, and these include sin. Sin brings condemnation in the heart, and condemnation steals joy. Remember, condemnation does not come from God.

> *There is therefore now no condemnation to them which are in Christ Jesus...*
>
> *Romans 8:1*

Sometimes, people may do things that can steal our joy, but we must fight against being kept in bondage of the fear of man. When we strive to please men, it can bring about disappointments and discouragement, which eventually steals our joy.

The fear of man bringeth a snare: but whoso putteth his trust in the LORD shall be safe.

Proverbs 29:25

Our trust must be in God, not man. When men do not perform as promised, they are just being human and as such, we do not need to take offence. If they could do better, they would have. The truth is: Man at his best is always **limited**! It is God that is unlimited; so, you can afford to trust Him whole-heartedly.

Thus saith the LORD; Cursed be the man that trusteth in man, and maketh flesh his arm, and whose heart departeth from the LORD.

Jeremiah 17:5

The pursuit of joy must become your priority in life. Therefore, endeavour to be a man or woman of joy.

Choosing to be joyful is an act of obedience

"Joy", in Hebrew, means rejoicing and gladness, while in Greek, it means cheerfulness. On the other hand, obedience is dutifully complying with the commands, orders or instructions of one in authority. It also means doing what you are told to do.

Being joyful as an act of obedience is simply being full of joy, irrespective of the circumstances or situations that you may be confronted with in life.

As expressed earlier in this book, joy is constant and not dependent on circumstances or mood. This joy comes from within us as children of God, because Christ lives in us. Joy can exist even in adverse situations or circumstances.

Someone said, "I find joy in everyday living. Not because life is always good, but because God is."

Please understand: Joy is deeper than happiness, because it is an inner attitude of rejoicing in one's salvation, regardless of the outward circumstances. This is why the believer is admonished to "rejoice evermore" (**1 Thessalonians 5:16**). Consequently, adhering to this instruction shows an act of obedience on our part.

When we obey this instruction from God, it is an indication of our absolute confidence in Him. Being joyful is a command, and adhering to it is obedience.

This kind of obedience is demonstrated in the way we behave, and our attitude will be evident in:

Following God's Word

David always demonstrated his joyfulness in God's Word.

> *I have rejoiced in the way of thy testimonies, as much as in all riches.*
>
> Psalm 119:14

Reading and meditating on God's Word was always David's delight. That is why he always drew strength from the counsel of the Lord in times of trouble. The Word was always his joy and source of strength. Obviously, the Word of God is one of the great streams of the river of joy.

> **The statutes of the LORD are right, rejoicing the heart: the commandment of the LORD is pure, enlightening the eyes.**
>
> Psalm 19:8

Trusting God

Trust means believing totally.

> **Now the God of hope fill you with all joy and peace in believing, that ye may abound in hope...**
>
> Romans 15:13

When we trust a person, we obey whatever that person

tells us to do, because we believe he or she will not lead us astray.

> *...but he that putteth his trust in me shall possess the land, and shall inherit my holy mountain.*
>
> *Isaiah 57:13*

Therefore, trusting in God and His Word is the result of joyfully believing His Word.

> *Some trust in chariots, and some in horses: but we will remember the name of the LORD our God.*
>
> *Psalm 20:7*

Putting our trust in God makes us obey His commandments, as our hearts will rest totally and confidently in Him. According to Joyce Meyer, "I believe that a trusting attitude and a patient attitude go hand in hand. You see, when you let go and learn to trust God, it releases joy into your life."

A trusting attitude keeps us joyful continually. This was Jesus' secret when He was to be crucified.

> *Looking unto Jesus ...who for the joy that was set before him endured the cross, despising the shame...*
>
> *Hebrews 12:2*

We are empowered by the Holy Spirit to sustain such joyfulness as an act of obedience.

Now the God of hope fill you with all joy ...through the power of the Holy Ghost.

Romans 15:13

Delighting in God's Presence

God's presence is always a source of joy.

Therefore my heart is glad, and my glory rejoiceth... in thy presence is fulness of joy...

Psalm 16:9-11

You cannot be in God's presence and remain downcast; His presence is a sure tonic for joy. When you carry God's presence in your life, you will be joyful always.

Understanding God's Word

Meditating on the Word causes our hearts to be full of God.

Thy words were found, and I did eat them; and thy word was unto me the joy and rejoicing of mine heart...

Jeremiah 15:16

God's Word stirs up faith in our spirit. We encounter this kind of faith when our spirit is illuminated by the Holy Spirit. This illumination is as a result of the light of the Word, which dispels darkness (life's situations and circumstances). This can be likened to the experience of Jonathan when he was hungry; and a taste of honey, obviously, brought refreshing to him.

Then said Jonathan...see...mine eyes have been enlightened, because I tasted a little of this honey.

1 Samuel 14:29

It is the understanding of God's Word that brings about illumination over darkness, which ultimately results in great joy. When the Word of God is resident in your heart, you are empowered to be joyful as an act of obedience.

And ... these things I speak in the world, that they might have my joy fulfilled in themselves.

John 17:13

Being a Peacemaker at all Times

Pursuing peace as a lifestyle requires a deliberate effort.

Blessed are the peacemakers: for they shall be called the children of God.

Matthew 5:9

This demands overlooking offences, forgiving easily, handling conflicts in a biblical way and seeking peace with all men. The hope we have is that God's grace enables us to resolve conflicts in a way that glorifies Him and preserves our precious relationships.

...to the counsellors of peace is joy.

Proverbs 12:20

Surrendering to God in Every Situation

To surrender to God is to allow ourselves to be controlled by Him.

Be still, and know that I am God...

Psalm 46:10

This means giving up our will to do things ourselves, and allowing God to take charge. This implies that we refuse to be self-reliant; rather, we acknowledge our weakness and look up to God for His strength. When we surrender all to Him, victory is sure and joy is the outcome.

Commit thy way unto the LORD ...and he shall bring it to pass.

Psalm 37:5

Hope in God at all Times

When your hope is in God, it means you are looking up to Him with expectation.

...He shall strengthen your heart, all ye that hope in the LORD.

Psalm 31:24

Joyful obedience is triggered by your hope in God. This is because you are confident that God will not abandon you. An example is Abraham, who hopefully maintained joy in obedience, as commanded.

Who against hope believed in hope, that he might become the father of many nations... was strong in faith, giving glory to God...

Romans 4:18-22

In the end, God fulfilled the promise by giving him Isaac. This is why you must keep hope in one hand and joy in the other.

Rejoicing in hope...

Romans 12:12

Being joyful as an act of obedience must also be evident in your worship of God as follows:

An Act of Worship to God

A man filled with joy will not be compelled to worship God. He constantly remembers God's faithfulness and therefore, remains grateful. He is joyful because his worship is an act of reverence to God.

Serve the LORD with gladness: come before his presence with singing.

Psalm 100:2

Serving Others with Delight

It takes a joyful heart to serve others with delight. Jesus demonstrated this by showing love to all equally.

Fulfil ...joy ...having the same love, being of one accord, of one mind.

Philippians 2:2

Abiding in Christ

A heart filled with joy will never give up on God because He is the Giver of joy. No matter the situation, such an individual will not give up because of his confidence in God's ability to change the situation; and as such, he abides in the Word.

Are you confronted with a challenging life situation right now? Don't give up on God!

...ye shall abide in my love ...that my joy might remain in you, and that your joy might be full.

John 15:10-11

Being Generous

It takes a heart of joy to give, especially if you have limited resources and you are in need.

Personally, one of the most exciting moments of my life is when I have an opportunity to give; not just giving my offerings to God, but also being a blessing to people through giving.

> *And he saw also a certain poor widow casting in thither two mites. And he said, Of a truth I say unto you, that this poor widow hath cast in more than they all...*
>
> Luke 21:2-4

It takes joy to give, especially, when it's not convenient. This was the testimony of the Macedonian Church in this scripture:

> *How that in a great trial of affliction the abundance of their joy and their deep poverty abounded unto the riches of their liberality.*
>
> 2 Corinthians 8:2

The benefits of being joyful as an act of obedience include:

Freedom from being controlled by material things

That is, the source of one's joy is not based on material things, but on God. Therefore, you cannot be controlled by material things.

37

But my God shall supply all your need according to his riches in glory by Christ Jesus.

Philippians 4:19

Freedom from Despair

Despair is a sign of hopelessness. A joyful heart is free of despair, because such a person is not looking at the present situation that may seem discouraging, but at the future that is full of glory. When you joyfully obey, you can't lose hope.

> *And being not weak in faith, he considered not his own body now dead, when he was about an hundred years old, neither yet the deadness of Sara's womb: He staggered not at the promise of God through unbelief; but was strong in faith, giving glory to God;*

Romans 4:19-20

Peace in our Waiting

Where there is joy, hope and patience are also present. A joyful heart will always have peace and patience, because God is the source of that joy.

> *And when he had consulted with the people, he appointed singers unto the LORD, and that should*

praise the beauty of holiness, as they went out before the army, and to say, Praise the LORD; for his mercy endureth for ever.

Then they returned, every man of Judah and Jerusalem, and Jehoshaphat in the forefront of them, to go again to Jerusalem with joy; for the LORD had made them to rejoice over their enemies.

2 Chronicles 20:21 & 27

Peace in and Through Trials

A joyful heart enjoys peace even in trials and tribulations, because his hope and trust is in God, Who will surely deliver from destruction.

And the LORD shall guide thee continually, and satisfy thy soul in drought, and make fat thy bones: and thou shalt be like a watered garden, and like a spring of water, whose waters fail not.

Isaiah 58:11

Freedom from Bitterness

Bitterness is holding on to a wrong done to you by someone. On the contrary, a joyful heart holds no wrong. Whenever the commandment of being joyful is obeyed, bitterness is rooted out.

39

A merry heart doeth good like a medicine: but a broken spirit drieth the bones.

Proverbs 17:22

Joy and Our Relationship With God

Joy comes from God

...behold, I bring you good tidings of great joy...

Luke 2:10-11

Without God, you cannot have joy and without joy, you cannot have a strong relationship with Him. So, you must give yourself to what it takes to maintain a heart full of joy.

Joy is enhanced by righteousness

But let the righteous be glad; let them rejoice before God: yea, let them exceedingly rejoice.

Psalm 68:3

Departure from sin must be your delight!

Joy increases because of our deeper relationship with God

For God giveth to a man that is good in his sight... joy...

Ecclesiastes 2:26

God has destined your life for joy. Therefore, as you seek God, study His Word and respond to the promptings of the Holy Spirit, you become more intimate with Him, and this brings about greater joy in your life.

"The fruits of the Spirit are spiritual forces that work much like antioxidants, renewing our youth, protecting us and defending us from the attacks of the devil."

- Gloria Copeland

3

Sources Of Joy

Shout aloud and sing for joy, people of Zion, for great is the Holy One of Israel among you.

Isaiah 12:6 (NIV)

The Almighty God is the source of this force called joy because that is His nature. God is our Progenitor and all divine virtues, including joy, flow from Him. Therefore, without God in your life, it is impossible to experience joy or remain joyful.

The question then is: How has God made Himself available to us, to connect with this flow of virtue?

The following reveal to us how we can connect with this great virtue of joy:

Through the Knowledge of God's Word

Joy is a force of the Spirit that has its source in our knowledge of God and His Word. The knowledge of God's Word has the ability to stir up joy in you at all times, even in adverse circumstances.

> ***Thy words were found, and I did eat them; and thy word was unto me the joy and rejoicing of mine heart...***
>
> *Jeremiah 15:16*

Please understand: The truths in God's Word are unveiled by the Holy Spirit. This kind of encounter is referred to as the revelation of the Word of God. It is **revelation** that can bring about a **revolution** and consequently, a **transformation** in your life.

When the light of God's Word shines in your heart, it brings about excitement and consequently, produces faith. This dimension of the Word is called *Rhema*. In other words, the Holy Spirit gives you a Word that is relevant for a specific situation.

It is this kind of knowledge of the Word that brings freedom and confidence.

> ***And ye shall know the truth, and the truth shall make you free.***
>
> *John 8:32*

44

Joy gives you an unwavering belief that God's Word will always be fulfilled, regardless of the circumstances.

God's Word contains good news. For instance, Jeremiah 29:11 (NIV) says:

For I know the plans I have for you," declares the LORD, "plans to prosper you and not to harm you, plans to give you hope and a future.

This is good news! God has plans for you. These plans will result in prosperity, ensure a great future, and protect you.

This is enough to bring a smile to your face! Just give it a thought: no matter what you are going through now, your future will surely be better! There is hope! Therefore, rejoice!

"Gospel" means good news, and it always stimulates joy and rejoicing. David compared the joy of discovering riches to discoveries in the Word.

He said:

I rejoice at thy word, as one that findeth great spoil.

Psalm 119:162

Just think of that! Imagine the level of excitement that wells up within a person who discovers that he has been bequeathed billions of dollars as an inheritance.

His walking style will change and there will be a song on his lips. Life will look different to such a person. That is the same thing that should happen to a believer when he receives insight from the Scripture.

Based on scriptures, there is no justifiable reason for a believer to be sorrowful.

Jesus said in John 16:33:

> *These things I have SPOKEN unto you, that in me ye might have PEACE. In the world ye shall have tribulation: BUT BE OF GOOD CHEER; I HAVE OVERCOME THE WORLD (Emphasis mine).*

This means that each time Jesus wants to release joy into your life, He speaks His Word. ***These things have I SPOKEN UNTO YOU...***

The Word of God is the greatest joy stimulant!

Through the Ministry of the Holy Spirit

The Holy Spirit is the Oil of joy. The Psalmist prophetically declared one of the virtues in the life of Jesus.

> *...God, has set you above ...by anointing you with the oil of joy.*
>
> Psalm 45:7 (NIV)

This virtue of joy in the life of Jesus was as a result of the anointing of the Holy Spirit.

How God anointed Jesus of Nazareth with the Holy Ghost...

Acts 10:38

That kind of Jesus' joy cannot be humanly produced, but by the Holy Spirit, Who is the Oil of joy. For instance, Jesus remained joyful on His way to the cross. It is written:

Looking unto Jesus... who for the joy that was set before him endured the cross, despising the shame...

Hebrews 12:2

It takes the Holy Spirit to produce this virtue of joy, which is also a fruit of the Spirit.

But the fruit of the Spirit is... joy...

Galatians 5:22

When baptised in the Holy Spirit, the virtue of joy is imparted into you. This is why joy is from within. It is in you like a spring, bubbling up and manifesting on the outside as joy.

Through Evangelism

I discovered that sharing the message of salvation releases joy into the life of the person evangelising. The Holy Spirit imparts joy and fulfilment when one

47

shares the good news of salvation with an unbeliever, especially when there is a positive response.

It is written:

And the seventy returned again with joy, saying, Lord, even the devils are subject unto us through thy name...

Luke 10:17-24

Definitely, there is a covenant connection between joy and sharing the good news of God's love to mankind.

Going out to evangelise can be very demanding, but when a soul responds to the good news of salvation, the story changes and it is worth all the effort. The convert is joyful and the person sharing the good news also experiences joy.

Personally, I experience this again and again. I encourage you to get involved in soul-winning and experience the joy that accompanies it! You will be glad you did – I guarantee you!

However, there is also joy in heaven when a sinner repents.

...joy shall be in heaven over one sinner that repenteth, more than over ninety and nine just persons...

Luke 15:7

As seen in the Scripture, Jesus rejoiced in the salvation of men when the disciples He sent out returned with the report of people responding to the good news.

...Jesus rejoiced in spirit, and said, I thank thee, O Father, Lord of heaven and earth...

Luke 10:21

It was God's "good pleasure" to accomplish the salvation of men through His Son, Jesus Christ. In this plan and purpose of God, Jesus made real the sovereign purposes of the Father with respect to the salvation of men, by giving Himself to pay the price for man's sin. This He did joyfully and in this role, Jesus' joy was not only subject to the will of God, but was founded on the will of God.

It was this joy that sustained Jesus Christ through His suffering on the cross (Hebrews 12:2).

This is why salvation brings joy into a man's life! In other words, joy always accompanies true salvation!

Clearly, Abraham's joy was in the coming of Christ. The Bible says:

Your father Abraham rejoiced to see my day: and he saw it, and was glad.

John 8:56

David's joy was the joy of salvation.

Restore unto me the joy of thy salvation...

Psalm 51:12

John the Baptist's joy was in the introduction of Jesus Christ.

He that hath the bride is the bridegroom: but the friend of the bridegroom, which standeth and heareth him, rejoiceth greatly because of the bridegroom's voice: this my joy therefore is fulfilled.

John 3:29

The Ethiopian Eunuch experienced joy when he encountered insights about the Saviour. The result was that he got saved and demonstrated his acceptance by being baptised in water by immersion immediately.

And when they were come up out of the water, the Spirit of the Lord caught away Philip, that the eunuch saw him no more: and he went on his way rejoicing.

Acts 8:39

The Philippine jailer's joy was as a result of him and his family's encounter with new birth.

And when he had brought them into his house, he set meat before them, and rejoiced, believing in God with all his house.

Acts 16:34

50

Above all, joy characterises the life of every true believer.

> *Thou wilt shew me the path of life: in thy presence is fulness of joy...*

Psalm 16:11

Why Do People Lack Joy?

If joy is one of the virtues that accompany salvation, then, why do very few Christians demonstrate it?

It may be because they have not experienced the salvation that produces it

"It is joyous to be saved," says Kenneth E. Hagin. Also, John Piper, in an excellent book titled, *Delighting In God*, suggests that the presence or absence of joy may be a better test of one's salvation than mere profession. He further states that if one does not really delight in God, His presence, His Word and His worship, then, one should really consider the validity of their profession of faith.

In other words, your attitude towards God and His Word is indicative of your spiritual state. If you are joyful, it means you have a vibrant spirit, which is alive to God. If not, you may need to re-examine your spiritual state. This is very important because when Christians backslide, the first sign is loss of joy.

Do you delight in God? Do you desire to pray, worship and study His Word? If not, your lack of joy may reflect the fact that you have not yet experienced His salvation or you are in a backslidden state.

Lack of joy in the life of a Christian may be the result of unconfessed sin

Unconfessed sin is the cloud that dims the rays of sun off His salvation.

David prayed in Psalm 51:12:

Restore unto me the joy of thy salvation...

This was the psalm of David when Nathan the prophet confronted him with his adulterous act with Bathsheba. Adultery and other immoral acts are sins in the sight of God, no matter who is guilty of them.

David needed to pray for forgiveness and that God should restore the "joy of His salvation".

When your life lacks joy as a Christian, you may need to examine yourself; perhaps, there is an unconfessed sin that needs to be settled.

If we say that we have no sin, we deceive ourselves,

and the truth is not in us.

If we confess our sins, he is faithful and just to forgive us our sins, and to cleanse us from all unrighteousness.

1 John 1:8-9

The solutions to unconfessed sins are confession and repentance.

Lack of joy in the life of a Christian may be the result of wrong focus

Lack of joy in a believer's life could be because their faith isn't firmly grounded in God and His Word. When the focal point of your desires is not God, the joy of your salvation diminishes. Where one's treasure is, that is where one's heart will be, and consequently, that will be where pleasure is derived.

For where your treasure is, there will your heart be also.

Matthew 6:21

Your treasure follows your investments of God-given resources of time, money and spiritual gifts. When you begin to take pleasure in things, rather than God's Word, the result is that you will misappropriate the things given to you as a steward, and the source of your pleasure will shift. This, eventually, weakens your joy in the Lord.

May God enable you to find your joy in Him and in Him alone!

"I strongly believe that if anyone cannot find joy in Christ, he can never find it anywhere else."
– Dr David O. Oyedepo

4

Dimensions Of Joy

...and many shouted aloud for joy:

So that the people could not discern the noise of the shout of joy...

Ezra 3:12-13

The New Testament clearly shows us how joy characterised the lives of Jesus' followers. Remember, joy is unaffected by circumstances because it is a force of the Spirit. Joy is naturally a fruit of a Spirit-led life as seen in the lives of the disciples, the brethren, the Philippine jailer, etc. The Christian-patterned joy, therefore, must be a product of our walk with God.

Some dimensions of joy seen in Scripture include the following:

Exceeding Joy

Then will I go unto the altar of God, unto God my exceeding joy: yea, upon the harp will I praise thee, O God my God.

Psalm 43:4

Evidently, God is the fountain of exceeding joy. No one can ever take the place of God in a man's life. Let this truth permeate your being and lift you up, because joy is a mystery weapon. Once you lay hold on it, the journey of life will be made cheap for you.

The Bible says in Matthew 2:10:

When they saw the star, they rejoiced with exceeding great joy.

Also, the birth of Jesus Christ was the complete answer to the world's ordeal. This, indeed, brought exceeding joy to man. There's no greater joy than knowing that someone cares for you unreservedly.

Carefully consider the following scriptures:

But rejoice, inasmuch as ye are partakers of Christ's sufferings; that, when his glory shall be revealed, ye may be glad also with exceeding joy.

1 Peter 4:13

Now unto him that is able to keep you from falling, and to present you faultless before the presence of his glory with exceeding joy.

Jude 1:24

Every child of God has a deposit of that special grace, which can enable them confront every challenge of life with exceeding joy. So, let your heart acknowledge and get acquainted with joy beyond what the world can afford, by dwelling on God's unquestionable love.

Joy Unspeakable

Whom having not seen, ye love; in whom, though now ye see him not, yet believing, ye rejoice with joy unspeakable and full of glory:

1 Peter 1:8

Hope in God is a living hope, which propels joy unspeakable. It enlivens and comforts in all distresses, which eventually enables us to overcome all difficulties of life. Joy unspeakable is not for the natural man, but for the man of the Spirit.

Obviously, people aren't always going to contribute

57

to your joy. Hence, let your focus be on God, for He alone can guarantee you joy inexplicable but undeniable. In other words, make God your only source of joy and He will give you your heart's desires.

Shared Joy

Apostle Paul experienced shared joy, as seen in his epistle to the Philippian Church, in the following account:

> *I thank my God upon every remembrance of you, Always in every prayer of mine for you all making request with joy, For your fellowship in the gospel from the first day until now;*
>
> *Even as it is meet for me to think this of you all, because I have you in my heart; inasmuch as both in my bonds, and in the defence and confirmation of the gospel, ye all are partakers of my grace.*
>
> *For God is my record, how greatly I long after you all in the bowels of Jesus Christ.*
>
> *Philippians 1:3-5, 7-8*

This partnership is more than just spending time together; it is a bond that makes us one big family in Christ. The following represents what we share as Christians:

- A Common Salvation

- A Common Grace

- A Common Burden

- A Common Hope

You are, therefore, encouraged to savour life by finding joy in the journey, and sharing same with brethren and family, as often as possible.

Confident Joy

This dimension of joy can be confided in, knowing that we cannot be put to shame trusting in the Lord, with declarations based on God's promises.

Which is the earnest of our inheritance until the redemption of the purchased possession, unto the praise of his glory.

Ephesians 1:14

In the experience of Paul, he made this statement as one of the greatest reasons for the joy we have, **being confident of this, that he who began a good work in you will carry it on to completion until the day of Christ Jesus** (Philippians 1:6, NIV).

Paul affirms in this scripture that God will finish what He started. This is such a significant truth. It is the basis of our confidence, peace and joy. God will definitely finish the good work that He has started in you – I guarantee you!

The Bible says:

> *What shall we then say to these things? If God be for us, who can be against us?*
>
> *He that spared not his own Son, but delivered him up for us all, how shall he not with him also freely give us all things?*
>
> *Nay, in all these things we are more than conquerors through him that loved us.*

Romans 8:31-32, 37

Put your confidence in Christ, and let nothing be strong enough to puncture your joy in the Lord.

Increasing Joy

The Christian joy is expected to deepen as we grow in our walk with God. So, it is actually an adventure that involves growth. As we grow in faith, our desires focus less on earth and more on Heaven, as our attitudes begin to portray more of Christ.

> *And this I pray, that your love may abound yet more and more in knowledge and in all judgment;*
>
> *That ye may approve things that are excellent; that ye may be sincere and without offence till the day of Christ;*

Being filled with the fruits of righteousness, which
are by Jesus Christ, unto the glory and praise of God.

Philippians 1:9-11

Paul's prayer was centred on the continuous growth of the believers' faith. Though they were sure of their destinies, yet, he felt the urge that they should also be progressing in the faith. The Christian life is not meant to be static, but progressive. We experience increasing joy, as we allow ourselves become more like Christ.

It is my earnest desire and prayer that you begin to experience increasing joy as you grow in the Lord.

Great Joy

After Philip preached in Samaria, the people believed and *there was great joy in that city* (Acts 8:8).

Also, the Scripture says:

Rejoice greatly, O daughter of Zion; shout, O
daughter of Jerusalem: behold, thy King cometh
unto thee: he is just, and having salvation; lowly,
and riding upon an ass, and upon a colt the foal of
an ass.

Zechariah 9:9

At salvation, a translation occurred from the kingdom of darkness to the Kingdom of light. You are no longer the same old being. In this new Kingdom, your past no longer affects your destiny; no matter how bad it was. Suddenly, all things have become new for you like a new born baby. This is exciting, great and wonderful; resulting in great joy!

Constant Joy

Philippians 4:4 says:

Rejoice in the Lord alway: and again I say, Rejoice.

Apostle Paul was never tired of stressing that joy is an important Christian trait. He emphasised that as believers, our joy remains constant when in God's presence, in communion with Him and in the understanding of Who He is. This is confirmed by the fact that God is always the same; His grace is always sufficient, His Blood has a continual virtue in it and always speaks for peace and pardon. Also, His righteousness and salvation are everlasting, and such is His love.

Thus, joy in God is of great consequence in a man's life, and Christians need to be continuously called to it. It outweighs the causes of sorrow, and it is a remedy for worldly tension.

The good news is: You can experience all these

dimensions of joy as a born-again Christian. However, these come when you love God more than anything the world has to offer. It is, therefore, wisdom to stop running away from God; rather, run to Him. Be restful in His grace and stop trying to pursue after uncertainties.

Receive God's gift of salvation, if you haven't, in order to qualify for these dimensions of joy, as they relate to your day-to-day life. Furthermore, be filled with the Holy Spirit, because joy is a fruit of the Spirit.

> "Joy cannot be masked; it is like a volcano, erupting into praise and dance."
> – **Faith A. Oyedepo**

5

Operating A Joyful Life

Rejoice, and be exceeding glad: for great is your reward in heaven...

Matthew 5:12

Joy has to be consciously generated. When joy is not flowing in your heart, it means a part of your heritage in Christ is missing. Therefore, you must consciously generate joy, in order to enjoy all the benefits of redemption.

However, before you can generate joy in your life,

certain conditions must be met. These are what I call prerequisites, and they include:

New Birth

According to Kenneth E. Hagin, "Joy is a fruit of the born-again, recreated human spirit." This attests that new birth is the impartation of a new nature, otherwise known as salvation. Except you are born again, you cannot connect with the Spirit of God that gives joy.

> *Therefore being justified by faith, we have peace with God through our Lord Jesus Christ ...and rejoice in hope of the glory of God.*
>
> *Romans 5:1-2*

Among others, two things happen at the point of salvation:

First, the life and nature of God (Zoe) is imparted into your spirit-man. You become a partaker of God's nature from which joy flows. The capacity to rejoice is imparted into you.

Secondly, you become the temple of God and thus, the Holy Spirit comes to reside in you permanently.

> *God is in the midst of her...*
>
> *Psalm 46:5*

When God is in you, then, you have the capacity and ability to generate joy always.

Holy Ghost Baptism

For the kingdom of God is not meat and drink; but righteousness, and peace, and joy in the Holy Ghost.

Romans 14:17

At salvation, man receives the capacity and ability to experience joy. However, at Holy Ghost baptism, we are empowered to be continually joyful.

And be not drunk with wine, wherein is excess; but be filled with the Spirit.

Ephesians 5:18

You get filled with the Spirit by "**Speaking to yourselves in psalms and hymns and spiritual songs, singing and making melody in your heart to the Lord**" (Ephesians 5:19).

When there is an infilling, there will always be a melody within you. Communion with the Holy Ghost always ensures joy is supplied continuously to believers. "Joy unspeakable, melody in your heart, will keep you winning," Dr David Oyedepo reaffirms.

Are you baptised in the Holy Ghost with the evidence of speaking in tongues? If not, this is the best time to do so!

Word Encounters

I rejoice at thy word, as one that findeth great spoil.

Psalm 119:162

God's Word gives us great joy more than how one rejoices when a box of treasures is discovered. This is why God gave us His Word to be continuously filled with joy.

...thy word was unto me the joy and rejoicing of mine heart...

Jeremiah 15:16

When God's Word becomes the joy and rejoicing of your heart, your life will never be dry of His praises.

To enjoy Word encounters, however, you must learn to camp with the Word of God consistently.

How to Consciously Generate Joy

With these prerequisites in place, the force of joy is put to work by consciously generating it. That is, you don't have to wait for joy to come; rather, you make it happen.

There are various steps to take in generating joy; they include, but are not limited to:

Make a decision to be joyful always

David said:

> **This is the day which the LORD hath made; we WILL rejoice and be glad in it.**
>
> Psalm 118:24 (Emphasis mine)

To be joyful requires a decision. Without a decision in place, you will become a victim of circumstances. David did not have the best of experiences at all times in his life, but he decided to rejoice and be glad, in spite of whatever may or may not have been happening.

Life is all about the choices we make; thus, we are products of our choices. If you want to be better tomorrow than today, you will need to make choices that will give you a better life and make you a better person. Whatever you are today is a product of your previous choices. Joy comes from the choices that we make in life.

> *I call heaven and earth to record this day against you, that I have set before you life and death,*

blessing and cursing: therefore choose life, that both thou and thy seed may live.

Deuteronomy 30:19

So, to rejoice is a choice. Jesus already made it clear that there shall be tribulations in life.

These things I have spoken unto you, that in me ye might have peace. In the world ye shall have tribulation: but be of good cheer; I have overcome the world.

John 16:33

Jesus also said that we should keep our joy, not just because of tribulations, but because He has provided a way of escape from every form of tribulation, so that it will eventually lead to our victory.

Obviously, your decisions in life lead to your destination. Whenever you decide to rejoice, you have chosen to ride on the highway of victory.

You can't continue to murmur and complain, and expect to flow in joy. From today, decide to rejoice always! History records that when Paul wrote to the Ephesians, admonishing them to rejoice, he was in prison. Rejoicing was his lifestyle and so, he could say:

Rejoice in the Lord alway: and again I say, Rejoice.

Philippians 4:4

Part of Paul's daily punishment in the prison was to be dipped into the town's central sewage holding. Notwithstanding, he still said, "**Rejoice evermore**" (1 Thessalonians 5:16).

It is your responsibility to generate joy around you; you cannot program sorrow and expect joy to surround you. So, make the quality choice to be ever joyful from today!

Ask for it

To generate joy, you must accept the responsibility to ask for it from God in prayers. The Scripture says:

...ye have not, because ye ask not.

James 4:2

Be confident that when you seek God in prayer for a baptism of the Spirit of joy, you definitely will receive it! Therefore, thank God because He wants us to experience joy at all times.

Listen to messages on joy and meditate on the Word

Surely, joy is your birthright in Christ, but you have a duty to make it happen. One of the ways to maintain your joy is by letting the Word of God dwell richly in your heart. As you continue listening to messages on joy, the Spirit of joy in the Word will eventually rub off on you.

> *And the spirit entered into me when he spake unto me...*
>
> *Ezekiel 2:2*

This also applies to reading and meditating on the Word. Reading the Scriptures will definitely boost your joy level.

Cultivate the habit of subjecting your emotions to the comfort of Scriptures

When you make the decision to be joyful always, you will be in control of your emotions, especially when confronted with unpleasant situations.

Evidently, God's Word, which is the Gospel, is good news. Through the eyes of the Scripture, there is always a way out of every adverse situation.

> *Blessed be God...Who comforteth us in all our tribulation, that we may be able to comfort them which are in any trouble, by the comfort wherewith we ourselves are comforted of God.*
>
> *2 Corinthians 1:3-4*

The Scripture is full of examples of men and women like us, who were confronted with adverse situations and came out victorious!

> *For whatsoever things were written aforetime were written for our learning, that we through patience and comfort of the scriptures might have hope.*

Romans 15:4

The Word of God is loaded with precious promises of His planned intervention in our affairs. Therefore, it is God's Word and not your feelings that should be allowed to be in control when you are challenged. Please be aware: Your negative feelings will always lead you into taking wrong decisions; therefore, resist the temptation to put your feelings above the Word of God!

Encourage yourself

David was a joyful king who understood how to continually encourage himself in the midst of challenges.

> *And David was greatly distressed; for the people spake of stoning him...but David encouraged himself in the LORD his God.*

1 Samuel 30:6

No wonder David was known to have fought so many battles, without losing any!

Encouraging yourself involves keeping your hope alive. A man without hope is like a blind man; it's impossible for such a man to see the future. One of the reasons you should keep your hope alive is because there is no situation impossible with God. David knew that though his wives and property were taken, the possibility of recovery was still there. That's why he was able to hear when God said, **"Pursue: for thou shalt surely overtake them and without fail recover all"** (1 Samuel 30:8).

Jesus, our perfect example, exhibited this attribute. The death of Lazarus could not affect His hope. With joy, He thanked God and called Lazarus forth.

...Jesus lifted up his eyes, and said, Father, I thank thee that thou hast heard me...when he thus had spoken, he cried with a loud voice, Lazarus, come forth.

John 11:41-43

Refuse to give room to sorrow by spreading negative news; rather, consciously generate joy around you.

Deliberately look for reasons to maintain joy

One way to encourage yourself is by recalling the faithfulness of God in the past, both in your life as well as in the lives of others.

The enemy tricks people by blinding their eyes to what God has done, and amplifies what is yet to be done. This way, you keep focusing on what you don't have and wonder if you have any reason to rejoice. The Bible says:

> **Bless the LORD, O my soul, and forget not all his benefits.**
>
> *Psalm 103:2*

Recounting God's faithfulness is a deliberate action. This is why you should look for reasons to maintain your joy.

The Psalmist said:

> **... I am so troubled that I cannot speak...I call to remembrance my song in the night; I meditate within my heart, And my spirit makes diligent search.**
>
> *Psalm 77:4-6 (NKJV)*

"Making a diligent search", as regards God's past blessings, demands that you remember His goodness in your life. As you think through, you will have cause to thank Him and this will generate joy in your heart. This gives an assurance of triumph.

I tell you: there is no solution in sorrow!

Keep company with joyful people

Paul was a man who knew how to keep company with joyful people. He said:

> ...*evil communications corrupt good manners.*
>
> 1 Corinthians 15:33

You will never maintain joy easily, if you keep company with depressed, murmuring and discontented people. This is because every association carries a particular spirit. It was written of Saul:

> ...*a company of prophets met him; and the Spirit of God came upon him, and he prophesied among them.*
>
> 1 Samuel 10:10

Therefore, stay away from people that murmur and complain because they will steal your joy! Rather, share joy with people that are joyful. An English Proverb says, "Joy that is shared is a joy made double."

76

Be a person of humour

It is rightly said that you have to sniff out joy, thereby keeping your nose to the joy trail. However, if you are to keep your nose on the joy trail, you must be humorous. Joy can be generated by creating humour around you and making it a lifestyle, for a humorous person is usually a joyful person.

Humour is the tendency to provoke laughter and produce amusement. In other words, one has the ability to create an environment that will make people around to laugh or get excited. Experiencing humour can, therefore, mean to be amused, laugh, or smile at something funny. Responding to humour makes you joyful, rather than being downcast.

People respond to humour by laughing, smiling or being amazed. A sense of humour helps you to turn unpleasant situations to fun and amusement. This gives the ability to laugh rather than frown, which eventually boosts your joy level.

A happy heart is good medicine and a cheerful mind works healing, but a broken spirit dries up the bones.

Proverbs 17:22 (AMP)

Therefore, we must always possess a sense of humour; otherwise, life will be full of unpleasant memories rather than pleasant ones. Let there be more joy and laughter in your life.

> *All the days of the desponding and afflicted are made evil [by anxious thoughts and forebodings], but he who has a glad heart has a continual feast [regardless of circumstances].*

> *Proverbs 15:15 (AMP)*

Yes, you can choose to smile always, no matter your situation. That is why being joyful is a personal choice! Therefore, make that choice today!

Operations of Joy

Joy is an essential factor in our day-to-day lives. It is even recognised medically as a good remedy for stress, whether you are young or old. The Bible also attests to this fact, as seen in Proverbs 17:22 (NIV):

> *A cheerful heart is good medicine...*

It has been proved scientifically that you cannot maintain muscle tension when you are laughing! It means that you cannot be joyful and not laugh. Clearly, joy is healthy; it destroys worries, reduces tension, increases production of endorphins, which are the body's natural painkillers.

To operate a life of joy, certain things must be in place. Let us examine some of them:

Recognise God as the true and only source of joy

This demands that you let your focus be on God; reioice in His works and ability to do all things.

Always possess an eternal perspective to life, as this is the key to a world of joy

As admonished by Apostle Paul in James 1:2, you must count it all joy when you encounter diverse situations, knowing that you have unending pleasures awaiting you in heaven.

Pray instead of worrying about your concerns

Worrying will not bring solution to any challenge; but prayer, definitely, will and actually does!

Make celebrating with others a way of life

Make other people's joy your joy. Follow the example of the angels, who experience joy over every sinner that repents (Luke 15:10). By so doing, you get excited always.

In Dr T.L. Osborn's words, "The desires that God has placed in you are vibrant proof that He destined your life for joy and great purpose." This is why there are certain truths we must know and understand about joy, in order to continually experience it, so we will not be robbed of our joy by reason of ignorance.

These facts include the following:

- Joy is not an emotion that can be forced, fabricated, or faked.

- Joy is not dependent on our circumstances. We can be in a complex situation and yet, experience joy.

- Joy is a product of being secured in the Lord.

- Joy comes when we have a clear purpose for our lives.

- Joy comes when we abide in God's presence.

- Joy comes when we praise God.

- Joy comes when we live an honest biblical life.

- Joy comes when we continually praise God for what He has already done.
- Joy comes when people see Christ in us.

Expressions of Joy

Obviously, joy cannot be hidden! Wherever there is joy, it always finds expression. Joy in your life can be expressed through:

The practice of generosity and compassion

Mother Teresa of Calcutta, who won the Nobel Prize for Peace in 1979, was undaunted in her daily desire to help those in need. She said, "Joy is a net of love by which you can catch souls." Mother Teresa's joy was inseparable from her love, compassion and generosity.

There is always a feeling of joy when you go out of your way to help others by being generous with your time, energy, skills, knowledge or financial contributions. Please understand: Just like faith, joy is a living force with unlimited capacity to grow. Joy grows out of practising reverence for life, and in embracing the inherent beauty that permeates all beings and nature.

A natural extension of showing kindness and gratitude

This force of joy is often characterised by the expression of excitement. Learn to be a grateful person – both to God and man. Make a habit of extending kindness as often as possible. Furthermore, joy is seen as a sincere smile. God-inspired or God-illuminated persons usually exhibit their joy with smiles. This inspires us to readily access the joyful peace they feel inwardly, as that which we desire ourselves.

Joy as the foundation of a spiritual life

Our Christian faith considers joy as our birthright and inherent condition of creation. Joy is the most infallible sign of the presence of God. Really, it is the foundation of a spiritual life. Jesus said:

> **These things have I spoken unto you, that my joy might remain in you, and that your joy might be full.**

> *John 15:11*

In Psalm 30:5 (NETB), the Bible says:

> **...One may experience sorrow during the night, but joy arrives in the morning.**

Our faith, acting as a refuge of grace in our day, is a

stepping-stone to joy and peace.

Therefore, receive grace to constantly operate a joyful life henceforth.

> "Joy is like love; it's not merely an emotion, it's a decision."
>
> – Kenneth E. Hagin

6

Joy And Faith Work Together

... I shall abide and continue with you all for your furtherance and joy of faith.

Philippians 1:25

Faith delivers on the platform of joyfulness. This is because when joy is in place, the thriving force of faith is energised to make things happen in our favour.

Although the fig tree shall not blossom, ...and there shall be no herd in the stalls:

Yet I will rejoice in the LORD, I will joy in ...God...

...my strength, and he will make my feet ...to walk upon mine high places.

Habakkuk 3:17-19

Joyfully expecting good things attracts good things into your life and in your direction. Indeed, what you expect creates a platform for what you experience.

Now the God of hope fill you with all joy...in believing, that ye may abound in hope, through the power of the Holy Ghost.

Romans 15:13

Joy operates with the expectation of good reports. When you are hopeful, you will keep being joyful and this enlists you amongst faith-filled believers, who cannot be defeated no matter the challenges of life.

Now faith is the substance of things hoped for, the evidence of things not seen.

For by it the elders obtained a good report.

Hebrews 11:1 - 2

Joy Fuels Faith

Joy ignites a force on your inside that propels you forward. It is this force within you that makes you defy the odds and overcome obstacles along your path. This is why every believer should be full of joy.

When your joy remains intact in the midst of difficulties, you will receive your heart's desires ultimately.

> *...if need be, ye are in heaviness through manifold temptations...yet believing, ye rejoice with joy unspeakable and full of glory: Receiving the end of your faith...*

> *1 Peter 1:6-9*

Joy Waters the Seed of Faith

Watering is required for every seed planted to germinate. Likewise, joy waters faith and leads us to our desired end as a result of our faith in God's Word.

Joy retrieves stolen property from the enemy's camp. This is because joy strengthens your persuasion and consequently your declarations, which in turn move God on your behalf.

> *...Yet I will rejoice in the LORD, I will joy in the God of my salvation. The LORD God is my strength, and he will make my feet like hinds' feet, and he will make me to walk upon mine high places.*

> *Habakkuk 3:17-19*

To be joyless is to allow the seed of faith in you to dry up. That shall not be your portion in Jesus' name!

The Covenant Connection Between Joy and Faith

No doubt, there is a covenant connection between joy and faith. Let us briefly examine this here:

Joy and Faith Deliver Sustainable Power

> *For there is hope of a tree, if it be cut down, that it will sprout again, and that the tender branch thereof will not cease.*
>
> *Job 14:7*

Joy is a major booster of hope, and hope works with faith. Faith gets stronger even when the expected miracle seems delayed. Without joy, faith is helpless. That is why no matter how fiery the messages of faith a man hears, if he is joy-dry, he remains helpless and sorrowful. So, joy empowers your faith supernaturally.

Joy and Faith Keep You Future-Focused

> *Who against hope believed in hope, that he might become the father of many nations; according to that which was spoken...*
>
> *Romans 4:18*

Abraham focused on the end, which was for him to become a father, even when himself and Sarah were already old and had passed the natural age of childbearing. Definitely, it takes joy to embrace the Word that holds the key to your future.

> *So shall my word be that goeth forth out of my mouth: it shall not return unto me void, but it shall accomplish that which I please, and it shall prosper in the thing whereto I sent it.*
>
> Isaiah 55:11

Faith is the ability to see the invisible, the better future that is ahead. One of the challenges many people are confronted with today is the inability to see a future in their present state. This is because it is often forgotten that the first step to rise from failure to success or from obscurity to limelight, is to see a better tomorrow. Joy helps to anticipate that better tomorrow and when that is the case, faith is kept alive.

> *...weeping may endure for a night, but joy cometh in the morning.*
>
> Psalm 30:5

Joy rejoices in the midst of challenges by helping you focus on your future and so does faith.

> *They that sow in tears shall reap in joy.*
>
> Psalm 126:5

Joy and Faith Bring Restoration

For there is hope of a tree, if it be cut down, that it will sprout again...

Job 14:7

Lazarus was already stinking by the fourth day after his death, and all hope seemed lost. However, when Jesus arrived on the scene, He first revived the joy that had withered away for over four days, by reason of sorrow.

Take a close look as this scripture:

Jesus saith unto her, Said I not unto thee, that, if thou wouldest believe, thou shouldest see the glory of God?

Then they took away the stone from the place where the dead was laid. And Jesus lifted up his eyes, and said, Father, I thank thee that thou hast heard me.

John 11:40-41

Lack of joy can keep a man in the grave of hopelessness. This is a state where faith cannot operate. Faith that will turn hopeless situations around functions where there is joy. Joy fertilises hope and hope fertilises faith. With joy, nothing becomes impossible to faith.

But without faith it is impossible to please him: for

90

he that cometh to God must believe that he is, and that he is a rewarder of them that diligently seek him.

Hebrews 11:6

Connecting Joy to Faith for Testimonies

To connect joy to faith, so as to birth testimonies, requires the following:

Be Rooted in God's Word

While we look not at the things which are seen, but at the things which are not seen: for the things which are seen are temporal; but the things which are not seen are eternal.

2 Corinthians 4:18

The adverse situations of life are temporary and are subject to change in the light of God's Word. Surely, God's Word never changes, but it has the capacity to change things. As long as you are rooted in the Word, the negative situations in your life are bound to change.

The process of building up your faith begins with the knowledge of God's Word. You have to be spiritually enlightened to operate faith and the joy of the Lord successfully in your Christian walk.

Think Your Way Up!

> *Come now, and let us reason together, saith the*
> *LORD...*

Isaiah 1:18

It is through careful reasoning of scriptures that words are converted to pictures. This was the strategy God gave Abraham, to possess the land He promised him.

> *And the LORD said unto Abram, after that Lot was*
> *separated from him, Lift up now thine eyes, and*
> *look from the place where thou art northward, and*
> *southward, and eastward, and westward:*
>
> *For all the land which thou seest, to thee will I give*
> *it, and to thy seed for ever.*

Genesis 13:14-15

Think through God's promises and visualise the Word in the light of the situation you are confronted with, for victory to become your portion. Remember:

> *This book of the law shall not depart out of thy*
> *mouth; but thou shalt meditate therein day and*
> *night...for then thou shalt make thy way prosperous,*
> *and then thou shalt have good success.*

Joshua 1:8

Maintain A Cheerful Countenance

The decision to be a person who lives each day in the joy of the Lord is one every believer must deliberately make.

This is the day which the LORD hath made; we will rejoice and be glad in it.

Psalm 118:24

Do not be so anxious about your future such that you cannot even enjoy today. The secret is to deliberately create joy around you by maintaining a cheerful countenance. A joyful person is one who is always glad, rejoices, celebrates, excited and never allows anything to discourage him. He maintains a heart that is always merry and consequently a cheerful countenance, no matter the situations or circumstances.

A merry heart maketh a cheerful countenance: but by sorrow of the heart the spirit is broken.

Proverbs 15:13

Therefore, no matter the situation, keep a cheerful countenance. A man without joy lacks the Spirit of God, because one of the fruits of the Spirit is joy.

But the fruit of the Spirit is...joy...

Galatians 5:22

93

Therefore, being a joyful person demands that you connect to the Giver of joy, the Holy Spirit. However, without a cheerful countenance, the Holy Spirit will not be attracted to dwell in you. Therefore, it is wisdom to choose to be cheerful!

"Joy is a natural human reaction to faith."
– Kenneth E. Hagin

7

Blessings of A Joyful Life

The LORD is my strength and my shield; my heart trusts in him, and I am helped. My heart leaps for joy and I will give thanks to him in song.

Psalm 28:7 (NIV)

Living as a joyful person provokes God's blessings upon your life. This is what makes it a mystery weapon in the hand of the saint. The result is that, life delivers triumph cheaply. Some of these blessings are as follows:

Joy is a Catalyst for Divine Presence

Joy in the heart will bring about praise, which provokes the presence of God. Praise is God's habitat, as He is always attracted to it.

...O thou that inhabitest the praises of Israel.

Psalm 22:3

With divine presence, nothing can harm you; you are secured from the enemy. What a blessing!

A vivid picture of this is painted by the Psalmist:

...Judah (praise) was his sanctuary ...The sea saw it, and fled: Jordan was driven back ...Tremble ...at the presence of the Lord, at the presence of the God of Jacob.

Psalm 114:1-7 (Emphasis mine)

Truth is: To be filled with joy is to be filled with God, and to be filled with God makes you triumphant. In the Scripture, Joseph is a practical example of a joyful and triumphant man. He served joyfully wherever he was found and as a result, the presence of God always brought him favour; consequently, he overcame every difficulty.

Read this scripture carefully:

And the LORD was with Joseph, and he was a prosperous man ...in the house of his master the Egyptian.

And his master saw that the LORD was with him, and that the LORD made all that he did to prosper in his hand.

And Joseph found grace in his sight...and he made

96

him overseer over his house...

But the LORD was with Joseph, and shewed him mercy, and gave him favour in the sight of the keeper of the prison.

And the keeper of the prison committed to Joseph's hand all the prisoners that were in the prison...

...Because the LORD was with him, and that which he did, the LORD made it to prosper.

Genesis 39:2-4, 21-23

Please understand that a sad countenance repels God's presence. That is why joy is one of the most distinctive evidences of the presence of God in a man's life. In other words, sad people are always prone to defeat.

A merry (joyful) heart doeth good like a medicine: but a broken (sad) spirit drieth the bones.

Proverbs 17:22 (Emphasis mine)

No matter the circumstances confronting you today, choose to be joyful and you will cheaply enjoy divine presence, which will in turn establish your desired victory.

Joy Gives Strength

The Patriarch, Kenneth Copeland, rightfully said, "Joy is that strength everybody's looking for." Really, the

97

more joyful you are, the stronger you become! This is a fact that is evident in Scripture:

> *...the joy of the LORD is your strength.*
>
> *Nehemiah 8:10*

This is because God designed joy to help you rely on His strength and not on your strength.

Joy releases every kind of strength you require in the journey of life; spiritual, mental and physical strength are available through the tonic of joy. Sadness weakens and drains you of creativity and motivation. This causes people to end up as non-achievers, which eventually make them suffer from depression, hopelessness and low self-esteem. This is why everyone needs the joy virtue in their lives. Indeed, joy is a sure source of strength!

Strength is needed in the three parts of man – spirit, soul and body:

Spiritual Strength

Spiritual strength is strength in the inner man or spirit; it is also referred to as inner strength. Inner strength is required to overcome temptations. Spiritual strength is contacted when you are joyful. This is why Joseph the joyful had strength to resist the lures from Potiphar's wife.

...and Potiphar's wife ...began to look at him lustfully. "Come and sleep with me," she demanded.

But Joseph refused...

She kept putting pressure on Joseph day after day, but he refused to sleep with her, and he kept out of her way as much as possible...

She came and grabbed him by his cloak, demanding, "Come on, sleep with me!" Joseph tore himself away ...as he ran from the house.

Genesis 39:6-12 (NLT)

The truth is: You cannot fight temptation without spiritual strength. If joy releases strength, then you cannot fight and win without joy.

Many people in life are already tired of fighting; they are struggling because they have lost their joy. The Bible says:

The vine is dried up, and the fig tree languisheth ...even all the trees of the field, are withered: because joy is withered away from the sons of men.

Joel 1:12

Therefore, if your desire is to win at all times, you must be joyful. This is because the more joyful you are, the more strength you receive from the Lord for victory.

Emotional Strength

Emotional strength is exhibited when you are in control of your feelings. This means that you are emotionally stable as you are not controlled by adverse circumstances of life.

Adverse life circumstances will always want to pull you in the direction of negative emotions, such as being downcast and sad. However, with emotional strength, you can harness your feelings in the right direction.

When our second son was born, we didn't have the finance for the kind of naming ceremony we desired, but we were joyful and excited. Imagine how as a young mother you are not able to entertain the guests that came to rejoice with you at the arrival of your new baby. Ironically, the baby was named Isaac, which means Laughter! Sure enough, the naming ceremony was a most exciting one, because it was characterised with laughter! Today, the story has changed positively. God has not only blessed us with more than enough for any kind of celebration, but we can afford to travel anywhere in the world to name our grandchildren. Truly, God is too faithful to fail!

It is time to take hold of your emotions, in order to celebrate a change of story in future. Joy is the way to enjoy emotional strength. With the understanding of who you are from God's Word, you are only permitted to obtain gladness and joy, while sorrow and mourning shall ultimately flee from you (Isaiah 51:11).

Physical Strength

Clearly, without joy in your life, you are rendered powerless. This is because joy evidently gives strength to the weak. When you allow the joy of the Lord to dominate your heart, weakness vanishes instantly, and you are supernaturally strengthened.

> *...neither be ye sorry; for the joy of the LORD is your strength.*
>
> *Nehemiah 8:10*

Physical strength is strength in the body, which is exhibited in a sickness-free life. Joy is a force of the Spirit that keeps you free from sickness, pains and discomfort in life. God has ordained that we live a joyful life, so we can be fit always and live a life of health and vitality.

A troubled heart is reflected in a sad countenance, and sickness thrives where there is sadness of heart. On the other hand, health and vitality are the results of continuous rejoicing.

> *A merry heart doeth good like a medicine: but a broken spirit drieth the bones.*
>
> *Proverbs 17:22*

It is a well-known fact that anxiety weighs a man down, which results in weakness and lack of self-motivation. It is written:

Anxiety in the heart of man causes depression...

Proverbs 12:25 (NKJV)

As long as you are depressed, you will become suppressed! Show me an excited fellow and you will see a bubbling fellow, full of life! Besides, joy is the weapon God uses to make believers strong.

Joy Ushers You into Realms of Insight

This is another blessing of a joyful life. Insight is the ability to see beyond the ordinary. With spiritual insight, you are able to disarm anything that wants to hurt you or threaten your peace.

They shall not hurt... for the earth shall be full of the knowledge of the LORD...

Isaiah 11:9

Insight is the revelation of knowledge, which results in a revolution.

However, connecting to insight results from a studious life and this is the product of being joyful. Just like a dead man cannot be taught in the grave, a sad heart cannot receive revelation.

Thus, to be sad is to be buried in the grave of hopelessness!

...with joy shall ye draw water out of the wells...

Isaiah 12:3

It is insight that makes you wise. This is why the Bible says:

Thou through thy commandments hast made me wiser than mine enemies...

Psalm 119:98

The more joyful you are, the wiser you become because it is with joy that you connect with the deep things of God. There is indisputably a supernatural access to the deep things of God, when you allow the joy of the Lord to fill your heart.

One of the deep truths you encounter from God's Word is His virtue of faithfulness. Your understanding of His faithfulness makes you trust Him completely, without a shadow of doubt. This gives you the assurance that God is in control and therefore, keeps you in peace. This quiet assurance makes you smile genuinely, your circumstances notwithstanding. No wonder the Bible says:

...keep in perfect peace him whose mind is steadfast, because he trusts in you. Trust in the LORD forever,

for the LORD, the LORD, is the Rock eternal.

Isaiah 26:3-4 (NIV)

It is wisdom, therefore, to relate with every discovery you make in the Word as reality. This way, nothing will be able to stop your joy once your heart is established on the integrity of the Word and the faithfulness of God.

Notably, every joyful saint enjoys supernatural wisdom! Joy cannot be separated from insight.

For instance, Apostle Paul was a man of unusual joy; he said:

...I rejoiced in the Lord greatly...

Philippians 4:10

As a result, he was Paul the insightful. He also said:

...through the abundance of the revelations...

2 Corinthians 12:7

Joy Makes for Supernatural Fruitfulness

A supernatural happening is one that is beyond natural understanding and cannot be explained by intellectualism; it can only be the hand of God. It is joy that moves God's hand to do inexplicable but undeniable things.

The Bible says:

...Let the people praise thee, O God... let the nations be glad and sing for joy... Then shall the earth yield her increase...

Psalm 67:1-7

Supernatural fruitfulness is the production of results that cannot be humanly explained.

Life is a seed. Anything we engage in, from which we expect a harvest, constitutes a seed. For instance, money is a seed; when you give it to the Lord or people, you have sown it and should anticipate a harvest. Material resources, kindness, attitude, time and energy are all seeds.

However, for these seeds to produce effectively, a required environment must be created. Likewise, an attitude of joy creates the right environment for fruitfulness.

The vine is dried up, and the fig tree languisheth... even all the trees of the field, are withered: because joy is withered...

Joel 1:12

When there is no joy, the environment becomes unfavourable, making the seed unproductive.

Child-bearing is a kind of marital fruitfulness. If you

believe God for the fruit of the womb, never allow the devil steal your joy. Else, if you keep frowning, you may be freezing your womb unknowingly, thereby making it unsafe for child-bearing. Therefore, loss of joy may result in freezing your bowels of fruitfulness without knowing. Please note: Supernatural fruitfulness is encountered and sustained by keeping a joyful disposition as a lifestyle.

Joy Keeps Your Hope Alive

Joyful people are always hopeful; as long as you are not hopeless, you cannot be helpless in life.

...rejoice in hope of the glory of God.

Romans 5:1-2

The first car we had as a family was a Volkswagen Beetle, which we rode with excitement and gratitude to God. The car broke down several times on the road, but we still maintained our joy and excitement, hopeful of a better future. Today, to the glory of God, the story is different as we can afford not only to ride the best cars but to also give such as seeds!

Certainly, you can't be hopeful without being joyful, because hope sparks off joy. Another attribute of hope is that it releases a new life on your inside that keeps you cheerful in the midst of trials.

Being hopeful is seeing the better future you desire becoming a reality and as such, you keep your joy by rejoicing all the time!

Rejoicing in hope...

Romans 12:12

No situation must be strong enough to rob you of the hope of a better tomorrow. When you become hopeless and do not see a better life in the nearest future, then, there is a very strong indication that joy is absent from your life. Your attitude should be that of praise and rejoicing, despite the negative or challenging situation that currently exists. With that attitude, hopelessness gives way to hope, which will eventually bring about a positive turnaround.

...Yet I will rejoice in the LORD, I will joy in the God of my salvation.

The LORD God is my strength, and he will make my feet like hinds' feet, and he will make me to walk upon mine high places.

Habakkuk 3:17-19

Joy Destroys Fear, Doubt and Anxiety

Joyful people do not fear, but rather overcome anxiety. They keep rejoicing and believing that God will surely do great things. Joy precedes the manifestation of great happenings. So, choose to remain excited and joyous always.

> *Fear not, O land; be glad and rejoice: for the LORD will do great things.*
>
> Joel 2:21

When my husband and I got married, there were days in our home that I had to manage the meagre resources available, as a wife and mother. I believed God for divine wisdom to know how to make the best use of what was available to feed my entire household. We had to improvise by eating food that was filling at dinner, in order to skip breakfast. But today, we eat whatever we desire at anytime and also have the privilege of being used of God to feed many! God is indeed faithful!

The truth is: If the devil cannot steal your joy, he cannot steal your miracles and blessings.

Note that being joyless is a miserable way to live and can make any man susceptible to oppressions of the devil. In other words, joy is evidently beneficial to our daily living.

Joy Guarantees Supernatural Harvest

"Harvest" signifies increase, multiplication and enlargement in a manner that glorifies God. It also signifies "gathering" or "bringing in" of large blessings.

The Bible talks about the weeks of harvest, when a farmer gathers the produce of the seeds he had previously sown.

...he ...appointed weeks of the harvest.

Jeremiah 5:24

Each time a farmer gathers harvest, he is happy at the result, as one seed can yield tens, hundreds and thousands of produce. This is multiplication of the original seed sown. This is why when we sow spiritual and physical seeds, we must expect multiple harvest. It is the joy of harvest that brings in our expectations.

You have multiplied the nation and increased its joy; They rejoice before You According to the joy of harvest, As men rejoice when they divide the spoil.

Isaiah 9:3 (NKJV)

Joy is the spiritual watering of the seed, in order to secure your harvest. It terminates toiling and sorrow in ploughing.

Also, joy destroys the threats to your harvest by eliminating the enemies of harvest, such as grumbling and complaining.

Furthermore, joy attracts angelic assistance. When

you rejoice in God's presence, the angels are at your command as they respond to the Word of God you declare.

> *...His angels, that excel in strength, that do his commandments, hearkening unto the voice of his word.*

Psalm 103:20

Joy also keeps you hopeful of a good harvest, as you excitedly expect and rejoice at the coming harvest. Invariably, Jesus rejoiced at the coming harvest of sons and daughters, who will be adopted as a result of laying down His life as a seed, for the salvation of many.

> *Looking unto Jesus ... who for the joy that was set before him endured the cross, despising the shame...consider him that endured such contradiction of sinners against himself, lest ye be wearied and faint in your minds.*

Hebrews 12:2-3

Therefore, be joyful for your time of harvest is sure!

> *Sing ... be joyful ... and break forth into singing ... for the LORD hath comforted his people...*

Isaiah 49:13

Joyful seeds produce undeniable supernatural harvest

in due season! Therefore, jealously guard your joy of harvest against joy-breakers.

"Joy is a mystery weapon. When you lay hold on it, life is made cheap for you."

– Dr David O. Oyedepo

8

Hindrances To Joy

...and no one can rob you of that joy.

John 16:22 (NLT)

In the Garden of Eden, Adam was saddled with two responsibilities – to dress and keep the garden.

And the LORD God took the man, and put him into the garden of Eden to dress it and to keep it.

Genesis 2:15

In the above scripture, the word "keep" means "to protect". Everything God gives man needs protection from the influence of the enemy; this includes the joy of the Lord. Adam failed to protect the garden and he lost it. If we fail to protect the joy of the Lord in our hearts, we stand the risk of losing it.

The enemy of the joy of the Lord in our lives is satan. However, he does not come in person to discourage us but through deceptive vices. That's why the Scripture says:

> **Lest Satan should get an advantage of us: for we are not ignorant of his devices.**
>
> *2 Corinthians 2:11*

However, the Bible admonishes:

> **Above all else, guard your heart, for it is the wellspring of life.**
>
> *Proverbs 4:23 (NIV)*

One of the virtues to jealously guard in our lives is the force of joy. We are to beware of the fiery darts of the wicked that can steal our joy.

> **...ye shall be able to quench all the fiery darts of the wicked.**
>
> *Ephesians 6:16*

Joyce Meyer, a joyful minister, said, "Watch out for joy-stealers: gossip, criticism, complaining, faultfinding and a negative, judgmental attitude." This means that there are some activities that if engaged in, can hinder joy in our lives.

Some of the fiery darts of the wicked that we should protect ourselves from include:

Negative Reports

The world is filled with bad news that flies around daily. In fact, it is commonly said that there is no news like bad news. Man, in his natural state will, most of the time, look at the negative first. If you fill a drinking glass half way with water and ask people to describe what they see, those who will say that the glass is half-empty will be more than those who will say that it is half-full.

Life is a function of perspective. Every negative report is simply another person's point of view that does not paint the whole picture.

Even though you may not be able to stop negative reports from flying around, you can stop it from entering into your heart. Any information that is contrary to the Word of God is a negative report.

Scripturally, how should we handle negative reports?

Consider the following:

Don't acknowledge them as the final say

Therefore take no thought, saying...

Matthew 6:31

The rule is: Never declare with your mouth any thought that you don't want to see happen in your life.

Cast them down and out immediately

Take a close look at this scripture:

Casting down imaginations, and every high thing that exalteth itself against the knowledge of God, and bringing into captivity every thought to the obedience of Christ.

2 Corinthians 10:5

Fill your mind with positive thoughts, especially scripturally based thoughts

Read this scripture carefully:

Finally, brethren, whatsoever things are true, whatsoever things are honest, whatsoever things are just, whatsoever things are pure, whatsoever things are lovely, whatsoever things are of good report; if there be any virtue, and if there be any praise, think on these things.

Philippians 4:8

Arrest all negative reports by the weapons listed above, in order to maintain your joy.

Fear

Fear is one of the hindrances to joy. Dwelling on negative reports will always breed fear. Moreover, harbouring fearful thoughts will open you up to the spirit of fear. There are some people that are afraid even when things appear alright; they fear that things may eventually go wrong. That is the spirit of fear at work!

Fear has an acronym that shows how weak it is:

False

Evidence

Appearing

Real

Fear is the exact opposite of faith. It empowers the confidence of the enemy and contaminates your faith. It is an expression of your confidence in the ability of the enemy to overcome you. Job describes fear best in Job 3:25:

> *For the thing which I greatly feared is come upon me, and that which I was afraid of is come unto me.*

The expression "fear not" appears in the Scripture 365 times, and there are 365 days in a year. This means, God has provided enough strength everyday of the year to overcome fear. Therefore, there is no reason to be afraid!

Murmuring and Complaining

Excessive dwelling on negative situations breeds murmuring and complaining.

The Bible commands:

> *Neither murmur ye, as some of them also murmured, and were destroyed of the destroyer.*
>
> 1 Corinthians 10:10

Those who murmured as the Israelites journeyed through the wilderness into Canaan perished on the way. Whatever negative circumstance you may be confronted with has an expiry date. However, when you complain, it becomes a hindrance.

Complainers always see only what is wrong. You cannot praise and complain at the same time. One of the reasons the Israelites complained in the wilderness was because, they easily forgot what God did for them in the past. When you fail to remember past victories and blessings, you become a victim of complaining and eventually become joyless. If we must be grateful, then we must always learn to recount past blessings of God.

...forget not all his benefits.

Psalm 103:2

Never allow past adverse experiences affect your future by destroying your joy in the present. You cannot do anything about the past; but the plan of the enemy is to make your future look like your past. Refuse to destroy the unborn colourful future by capitalising on your negative past experiences. Your future is so great; don't allow the enemy to destroy it through murmuring and complaining.

> *Remember ye not the former things, neither consider the things of old.*
>
> *Behold, I will do a new thing; now it shall spring forth; shall ye not know it? I will even make a way in the wilderness, and rivers in the desert.*

Isaiah 43:18-19

Discontentment

To a joyless person, nothing God does is worthy of appreciation or gratitude. To a person who murmurs and complains, God has never done enough.

The truth is: The blessings of God come into our lives in phases.

> *By little and little I will drive them out from before thee, until thou be increased, and inherit the land.*

Exodus 23:30

God expects us to be grateful at each level, but it takes joy to appreciate Him at each level.

The Scripture clearly states:

But godliness with contentment is great gain.

1 Timothy 6:6

Discontentment steals your joy, but contentment enhances it; learn to be contented!

Hopelessness

Lack of joy usually leads to lack of hope, but joyful people always have hope. It is important to keep hope alive, as hopelessness is an enemy of joy.

A life that is hopeless is a life that dwells in unbelief. Such individual believe that whatever he does will not succeed. It is a heart that is discouraged and never thinks any good can come out of a situation. It is a heart that lacks confidence in the faithfulness of the Word of God. The spirit of such individual is broken; this is a joy-killer. The Bible says that a broken spirit dries the bones (Proverbs 17:22b).

Hopelessness comes from a feeling of lack of faith and trust in God. When you find it difficult to believe that God can help you, then you submit yourself to hopelessness and depression, which takes joy far from you. Let not your hope be dashed, trust in God, and He shall strengthen your heart (Psalm 27:14).

Meditate on this scripture:

> *Be of good courage, and he shall strengthen your heart, all ye that hope in the LORD.*
>
> Psalm 31:24

Comparison

Comparison is the thief of joy. The truth is: You are unique, one of a kind! We are called to run an individual race; therefore, we do not need to compare ourselves with others.

> *For we dare not ... compare ourselves with some... comparing themselves among themselves, are not wise.*
>
> 2 Corinthians 10:12

Comparing yourself with others can bring about dissatisfaction, which leads to anxiety about life. This is why comparison is the game of fools!

When you engage in comparing yourself with others, it results in a whirlwind of worry and confusion.

If you engage in worrying about your future, you will rob yourself of the joy of today. In order not to allow this enemy (worry) steal your joy, you must stop comparing yourself with others or trying to figure out why things are the way they are.

Quit anxiously searching for an answer to that situation; rather, put your hope and trust in God, Who is all-knowing. Someone once said, "Why, God, why" and "when, God, when?" are two statements that get us frustrated and prevent us from enjoying the good life Jesus died to give us."

Therefore, quit being anxious! Stop comparing yourself with others!

Spirit of Heaviness

The Israelites became plagued with the spirit of heaviness as a result of their prolonged stay in Babylon, the place of captivity. This, we can deduce from the song they sang:

> *By the rivers of Babylon, there we sat down, yea, we wept, when we remembered Zion. WE HANGED OUR HARPS...How shall we sing...*

> *Psalm 137:1-4 (Emphasis mine)*

Heaviness is a spirit that seeks to steal people's joy. One way the spirit of heaviness gets a hold on people is by complicating simple issues. Having the tendency to complicate things is an enemy of our joy. You must learn to keep life as simple as possible, by not getting yourself worked up over little matters. You may have plans for your life, but you must always learn to follow God's directives per time.

> *The Spirit of the Lord GOD is upon me; because the LORD hath anointed me ... to give... the oil of joy for mourning, the garment of praise for the spirit of heaviness...*
>
> *Isaiah 61:1-3*

Many lose their joy because they make a big deal out of things that could be simple, fun, easy and even inexpensive, thereby giving room to the spirit of heaviness. Simplicity brings power, peace and joy. Therefore, learn to have a simple approach to life and keep the spirit of heaviness off your destiny.

"Comparison is the thief of joy."
- Theodore Roosevelt

9

Joy Boosters

Now the God of hope fill you with all joy...

Romans 15:13

There are some factors that help to boost joy in the lives of believers. They energise joy to keep it perpetually on the increase. They include, but are not limited to:

Keeping Your Hope Alive

Rejoicing in hope...

Romans 12:12

When our hope is alive, joy is increased in our lives. This is because we have the assurance that no matter the situation, our God is always faithful to take us to our desired place of victory. When a man has hope, he is not moved by negative circumstances he is confronted with. No matter how challenging, he will rather be joyful.

The truth is: Whenever there is hope, there is a reason to rejoice. Let nothing tamper with your hope, because it is the fountain of joy. A person with hope will go to church one more time, pray one more time, praise one more time, give one more time, and trust God one more time. Alleluia!

It is the Word of God revealed by the Holy Spirit that stabilises the heart and fuels hope in the inner man. For instance, hope kept Job through the period of great challenges (Job 14:7-9). Also, Abraham's hope kept his faith and joy alive, which consequently revived his physical body (Romans 4:18-21).

God's Word undeniably keeps hope alive, until promises become realities. Whatever cannot stop you from being hopeful cannot stop you from rejoicing. As long as you are hopeful, you will be joyful. Jesus, our perfect example, joyfully endured the cross, despising the shame (Hebrews 12:2). Therefore, keep celebrating your hope and you will keep being joyful. To be joyless is to be helpless.

Recalling Testimonies of God's Faithfulness

Another word for "testimony" is "good news" and anything good boosts a man's joy level. Testimonies are proofs of God's faithfulness on the earth; thus, they should be given attention and celebrated. A testimony is an evidence of what God did in the past, and a prophetic pointer to what He can do in the present and future, if given room.

> *Jesus Christ the same yesterday, and to day, and for ever.*

> *Hebrews 13:8*

Indeed, testimonies are prophetic seeds. The Psalmist knew this and that was why he said:

> *I have rejoiced in the way of thy testimonies, as much as in all riches.*

> *Thy testimonies also are my delight and my counsellors.*
> *Psalm 119:14, 24*

Testimonies are also prophetic arrows and that's why each testimony shared has the ability to reproduce.

The Scripture says:

> *... for the testimony of Jesus is the spirit of prophecy.*

> *Revelation 19:10*

Maintaining Excitement and Enthusiasm in Your Assignment

Jesus is a perfect example of One who maintained enthusiasm on His assignment, even at crucifixion.

...who for the joy that was set before him endured the cross, despising the shame...

Hebrews 12:2

The thought of fulfilling divine plan and assignment should keep your joy fuelled.

The assignment you pursue is as a result of the future you see. Enthusiasm is easily maintained when the goal is clear. This is why dreams about the future go a long way in sustaining enthusiasm. To be without a dream is to be without life; that makes such individual a wanderer instead of a wonder. That shall not be your portion in Jesus' name!

Once you discover your assignment in life, it is wisdom to maintain excitement and enthusiasm in its pursuit; this will definitely boost your joy.

Maintaining a Lifestyle of Praise

As long as your joy is intact, your destiny is intact. An atmosphere of praise and rejoicing keeps your joy on the increase.

According to Dr David Oyedepo, "You must first be thankful before you can be joyful, and you must be joyful before you can sing; otherwise, your song becomes mere noise."

Indeed, praise is an invitation that God cannot resist! Psalm 22:3 explains that where the presence of God is, there is fullness of joy. A heart of gratitude moves the hand of God to work in your favour, and when God works in your favour, joy is stirred up.

When you thank God for what He has done for you, it will propel Him to do more. Therefore, a heart that is always grateful is a heart that is joyful, because such individual sees every reason to thank God for what He has done.

Speaking to yourselves in psalms and hymns and spiritual songs, singing and making melody in your heart to the Lord.

Ephesians 5:19

Make praise a lifestyle and your joy shall be enhanced.

How Do You Praise God Effectively?

Praise is an act you consciously make happen. However, it begins with being joyful. When you are intoxicated with joy, it explodes in praises. There are conditions to be fulfilled, if your praise will be acceptable to God and not be mere noise.

> *Take thou away from me the noise of thy songs; for I will not hear the melody of thy viols.*
>
> *Amos 5:23*

The following are some of the conditions for acceptable praise:

Gladness of Heart

Without gladness of heart, the spirit of heaviness will take over.

> *Serve the LORD with gladness: come before his presence with singing.*
>
> *Psalm 100:2*

Praising God without gladness is likened to noise making, which is unacceptable to God.

> *Because thou servedst not the LORD thy God with joyfulness, and with gladness of heart, for the abundance of all things; Therefore shalt thou serve thine enemies...*
>
> *Deuteronomy 28:47-48*

Choose to be joyful, in spite of the challenges you are confronted with. Let the joy of the Lord be constantly seen in you. The life of a true Christian should be characterised by continuous celebration that serves as a prelude to eternal life.

Stay Connected to God

The Bible says:

For to him that is joined to all the living there is hope: for a living dog is better than a dead lion.

Ecclesiastes 9:4

Staying connected helps to build confidence in God. "Confidence" means absolute faith and trust in God. It is standing on God's Word and His promises in times of difficulty. When you remain confident of who you are in Christ, your joy constantly increases.

When you build your confidence in God, joy unspeakable is stirred up. To enhance your joy, stay connected to God at all times, your circumstances notwithstanding. People who have their confidence in God are naturally joyful.

Maintain Fellowship in Zion

Blessed are they that dwell in thy house: they will be still praising thee.

They go from strength to strength, every one of them in Zion appeareth before God.

Psalm 84:4, 7

To be continually joyful, consider the following helpful hints:

Be Given to Laughter

Laughter is said to be the best medicine. Science has proved that it takes more work for the facial muscles to frown than to smile! Notably, God also laughs:

He that sitteth in the heavens shall laugh...

Psalm 2:4

"To laugh" means to make sounds and movements on your face that show you are happy. This could also be referred to as having a sense of humour. Keeping an excited environment and heart will cause your joy to always be on the increase. When you keep your countenance and environment excited, depression is kept far from you, for wherever there is depression, there can be no joy. Therefore, no matter the situation, learn to laugh regularly!

Also, being quick to forgive others, when they offend you, helps to maintain a life of joy. Unforgiveness robs you of maintaining peace with people around you. Joy is increased in our lives when we learn to forgive and forget. Keeping a record of past offences reopens fresh wounds, feeds pains and hurts, which in turn fosters unforgiveness. If you want joy to be continually effective in your life, then you must learn to forgive and let go of offences.

Be Focused

"To be focused" is to be "single-eyed". This means to concentrate on something. It has been said that you give strength and momentum to whatever you focus your attention on.

The Bible says:

> *...if therefore thine eye be single, thy whole body shall be full of light.*

Matthew 6:22

Actually, maximum focus creates maximum impact. When you lose focus, you lose your force. When you lose force, you lose joy and enthusiasm in the process. It is wisdom to stay focused on the good things in life. Refuse to dwell on negative things or the past. Whenever one door closes, God has plans for the next door to open. However, focusing on the good is what opens the next door.

Goals demand total attention and as such, you must remain focused to attain them. To submit to distraction is to forfeit your strength and joy, but to remain focused

The Force Of Joy

is to gain mastery. When you focus on God's Word, you remain joyful and you are sure to emerge victorious.

Be Content

The word "content" is defined as "rest or quietness of the mind in the present condition; satisfaction which puts the mind at rest, and often implying a moderate degree of happiness."

Contentment can be said to be a decision to be happy and satisfied in your present position and with what you have. For your joy to remain on the increase, you must learn to be content. Contentment is worth more than all the material possessions you could possibly accumulate in a lifetime.

My husband, Dr David Oyedepo has rightly said, "Whatever God cannot give me, may I never have it; wherever God cannot take me to, may I never get there." That is a contented life! Sometimes, many people want something desperately and they try to get it for themselves by all means and at all cost, instead of trusting God for it.

However, such usually leads to worries to say the least, especially when things do not work out as expected. As a result, they lose their joy.

A heart that is contented will always be grateful and

rejoice irrespective of what he/she has, whether little or much; and this will keep joy perpetually on the increase.

> "Your joy comes from your relationship with the Lord – poured into your life as you abide in the love of God!"
>
> **– Gloria Copeland**

10

Be Joyful

Rejoice in the Lord alway: and again I say, Rejoice.

Philippians 4:4

The above scripture makes it clear that as believers, God commands us to be joyful. However, joy is a product of the workings of the Holy Spirit in the life of a believer, and it is a major prerequisite in acceptable service to God.

Serve the Lord with gladness...

Psalm 100:2

Joy can override discouragements and disappointments in life. Being a joyful person makes you an example of a true believer.

The truth is: Joy is what you always have to work at; it is not automatic. This is why we need the Spirit of joy.

At new birth, you become the temple of God and the Holy Spirit comes to reside in you.

The Bible says:

> *Know ye not that ye are the temple of God, and that the Spirit of God dwelleth in you?*

> *1 Corinthians 3:16*

Romans 14:17 then says:

> *For the kingdom of God is not meat and drink; but righteousness, and peace, and joy in the Holy Ghost.*

What this means is that, every virtue available in this Kingdom is accessible through the ministry of the Holy Ghost; He is God's provision for a life of endless joy. That is why neglecting the Holy Ghost and His ministry will result in a life of frustration.

It is impossible to live a life of joy in the energy of the flesh. That is why our heavenly Father gave us the Holy Spirit, Who intoxicates us with joy. The Bible used words such as "laughter" and "pleasure from wine and merriment", in association with joy.

> *I said in mine heart, Go to now, I will prove thee*

with mirth, therefore enjoy pleasure: and, behold, this also is vanity.

Ecclesiastes 2:1

In the world, men resort to drinking in order to forget their troubles, at least temporarily; they indulge in wine to feel good. However, in God's Kingdom, we resort to the wine of the Spirit.

In Ephesians 5:18, the Bible says:

And be not drunk with wine, wherein is excess; but be filled with the Spirit.

The Holy Spirit is *the wine of the Spirit!*

And wine that maketh glad the heart of man...

Psalm 104:15

The Holy Spirit is also referred to as **the Oil of joy**.

To appoint unto them that mourn in Zion, to give unto them beauty for ashes, the oil of joy for mourning, the garment of praise for the spirit of heaviness; that they might be called trees of righteousness, the planting of the LORD, that he might be glorified.

Isaiah 61:3

He is further referred to as **the Oil of gladness**, and He is the One that impart believers with joy.

139

Thou lovest righteousness, and hatest wickedness: therefore God, thy God, hath anointed thee with the oil of gladness above thy fellows.

Psalm 45:7

Please note: When you entertain sorrow, you invite the devil, as God cannot inhabit a joyless environment. The oil of joy is the cure for sorrow, grief and unhappiness.

After over 40 years of knowing God's servant, Dr David Oyedepo, intimately, I can say with every sense of responsibility that one of the components of the Spirit of God at work in his life, without any doubt, is the Spirit of joy.

On our wedding day, the officiating minister arrived late for Church service. Rather than get upset or disturbed, my husband quickly sought for a well-dressed brother to commence the service!

He is always excited and joyful; he is a man that has no downtime in life, a man of humour. No matter the situation, he is always joyful; no wonder, he is ever-winning.

However, desperation is a covenant requirement for impartation of the Spirit of joy. "Desperation" refers to the intensity of your desire. It is being ready to pay the price, go the extra mile, and taking any covenant step that may be required for the realisation of your desire. This demands focus, thirst and hunger for God, in addition to sensitivity. **Jacob** was desperate for a change, and he got it as a result of his desperation.

> *And he said, Let me go, for the day breaketh. And he said, I will not let thee go, except thou bless me.*
>
> *Genesis 32:26*

Elisha was desperate for a double portion of the anointing upon his master, Elijah, and did not let him out of his sight; he got it.

> *... Elijah said unto him, Tarry, I pray thee, here; for the LORD hath sent me to Jordan. And he said, As the LORD liveth, and as thy soul liveth, I will not leave thee. And they two went on.*
>
> *2 Kings 2:6*

Blind Bartimaeus desperately wanted his eyes to be opened and in his desperation, he cried out to Jesus for help; he also got it.

> *And when he heard that it was Jesus of Nazareth, he began to cry out, and say, Jesus, thou Son of David, have mercy on me.*
>
> *Mark 10:47*

Also, **the woman with the issue of blood** in her weak state was determined as she said: *...If I touch but his* *garments, I shall be made whole* (Mark 5:28, ASV). She did and was made whole.

So was **Hannah**:

And it came to pass, as she continued praying before the LORD, that Eli marked her mouth.

1 Samuel 1:12

Please understand: The Holy Spirit imparts us with joy. He also sustains joy in us and aids in developing the fruit of joy in the lives of believers, if only we desire and desperately pursue it.

"Joy gives you a kind of staying power that will make you a winner again and again."
– **Kenneth Copeland**

11

Some Joy-Provoked Testimonies

...the testimony of the LORD is sure...

Psalm 19:7

In this chapter, I have compiled some joy-provoked testimonies, to help inspire you to lay hold on yours.

What is testimony? The word "testimony" means "a witness". It is what you have heard and/or seen God do in your life or that of others. It is an undeniable act of God!

Testimonies are living examples of the gospel; they are more potent than words. Testimonies are prophetic pointers to divine solutions; they eliminate trials. This is one of the great tools Jesus and His disciples used to confirm that the words they spoke were true.

It's quite difficult for people to argue against the truth of another's experience, especially with proofs. Luke 21:12 says that you shall be tested and tried, but verse 13 says that it shall turn to you for a testimony. That is why whenever your faith is challenged, you should rejoice that the Lord has given you such a powerful weapon as testimony, which turns saints to overcomers on earth. It will, certainly, kick-start your overcoming results too.

...for the testimony of Jesus is the spirit of prophecy.

Revelation 19:10

For you to appropriately key into the mystery of testimonies as seen in the scripture above, let's briefly examine some important steps that will help you to maximise your understanding of them:

First: Take note of whatever catches your attention in each testimony, either by underlining or writing it down in a separate note. This exercise will help you to remember the details of God's doings, and it could be initiated by:

Who was involved in the process?

What God saved him/her from, and

What it felt like to take that step or make the decision that led to the said testimony.

Second: Recognise how God was involved in the process of the testimony by identifying:

What you learnt from those situations, and

The scriptural principles the testifier applied that helped him/her through those events.

Third: Meditate on steps one and two as analysed above. This is a spiritual process to be done in partnership with the Holy Spirit; so you need patience, sensitivity and open-mindedness. This step also empowers you to believe what you have identified and taken note of, which automatically turns you to an overcomer and inevitably, a living wonder.

As a result of these truths, I've dedicated this chapter to recount the faithfulness of God in the lives of people who tapped into the ceaseless flow of joy, as discussed in previous chapters of this book. Remember, David shot testimony arrows at Goliath and cut off his head (1 Samuel 17:37). Therefore, I'm expecting these testimonies to make profound impact on your life, as you go through them with an open heart.

Six-Year Fibroid Gone!

I got married in 2005, but could not conceive because I had fibroid and painful menstrual periods.

I had an encounter with God while reading the book, Signs and Wonders Today, authored by Dr David Oyedepo. Thereafter, I was convinced that my case was settled, but I didn't know how to build my faith.

During one of the nights in Shiloh 2009, I had a dream, where Pastor (Mrs.) Faith Oyedepo prayed for me, and said my case was simple and curable. She told me to get the book, The Law of Faith, authored by Dr David Oyedepo. When I woke up, I started feeding on that book as instructed.

While ministering on The Eleventh Hour Miracle in December, Dr David Oyedepo said, 'No matter how complicated your case is, there is a solution.' So, I **acquired the Spirit of joy**.

*To the glory of God, I won that battle! Today, the fibroid and painful menstrual periods are gone and I am pregnant! –***Mariehellen, K.**

Miracle Baby!

In 2012, I was gloriously married as prophesied by Dr David Oyedepo, during the Miracle Marriage Services of that year. I got pregnant immediately but after three months, I had a miscarriage. I came to Shiloh 2012 bleeding and in pains, but during Pastor (Mrs.) Faith Oyedepo's message on The Spirit of Joy, **God**

strengthened me.

On February 23, 2013, we offered our home as a Winners' Satellite Fellowship (WSF) centre; I believe that was the beginning of our testimony.

As the WSF Operators' Meeting on Easter Monday was rounding off, Dr David Oyedepo kept saying, 'Jesus appeared for 40 days after His resurrection; He will appear to you!'

On the 38th day, Jesus truly appeared to me, because I missed my period. Nine months later, I delivered my miracle baby. Praise the Lord! –**Olayiwola, A.**

24 Years Barrenness Destroyed!

We have been married for 24 years. I had 20 miscarriages and one still birth.

We keyed in to the Word of God that says God shall bless our bread and water when we serve Him. We got involved in Kingdom service, wrote the names of our babies and gave offerings on their behalf, for over 12 years.

During one of the services, Dr David Oyedepo said, 'It is with joy that you draw water out of the wells of salvation.' When my husband and I got home that day, **we decided to be happy and joyful, no matter what**. We held hands and prayed for grace to always be joyful, and God proved Himself faithful.

Today, we have our miracle baby in our hands. Thank you Jesus! –Pst. & Mrs. Ladun

15 Years Career Stagnation Destroyed!

In December 1997, I lost my job in one of the media houses in Nigeria. I started borrowing money to make ends meet. I did businesses with borrowed money, but they collapsed.

Last year November, I ran away from home because I was heavily indebted. Then, God instructed me to come to this Church and He would restore my glory. The next day, being Sunday, I prepared to come to Canaanland, and a Pastor gave me a free ride to church.

When we were about to enter Canaanland gate, I told him I was a first timer. Immediately he said, 'You are welcome to the arena of millionaires.' As he said that, **my lost joy was restored.**

During the 21-day prayer and fasting, Dr David Oyedepo declared that we should observe a week of praise and worship in our homes. I obeyed! Since then, God has been performing wonders in my life. In January, I got a stress-free job in one of the reputable television stations as Chief Writer and the package was very amazing.

This month, God gave me my own car. I formerly came

to church in other peoples' cars, but now, I have mine. I thank the God of this Commission for taking me out of the pit and placing my feet on a solid rock! **–Olabisi, T.**

Pregnancy Test Positive!

After I saw my menstrual period last month, I was worried. Then I was directed to read an article on Pastor (Mrs.) Faith Oyedepo's website – faithoyedepo.org. It was about the blessings of marriage captioned, Be Fruitful.

After reading it, I decided not to panic anymore, because **I understood** that children are our inheritance from our Father and **that worrying and fear would take me nowhere.** So, I decided to praise God at all times. I believed every word I read from that article, and claimed God's promises.

Thereafter, my husband and I went to see a doctor and the pregnancy test was positive! Praise be to the God of David and Faith Oyedepo! Our God is faithful! I surely know that whatever God does is permanent. Amen! **–Mrs. U. (Europe)**

15 Years Impotence Gone!

In 1998, I discovered that I had an erectile dysfunction, which later became full-blown impotence. Since then, I believed God for my healing.

I went to so many places and hospitals for treatment, but to no avail. However, the Holy Spirit kept telling me that as long as God lives, things would be okay.

*On November 1, 2013, I sent a text message to one of the pastors who taught me at the Word of Faith Bible Institute (WOFBI), and to the Church rescue line. Through them, I was privileged to meet with Dr David Oyedepo. He laid hands on me and prayed that I be delivered from that assault. **I was filled with joy** and I gave thanks to God.*

At the end of Shiloh, before I got to the gate, I had an erection. I give God the glory! –**Oselokhale, I.**

Ceased Menstrual Flow Restored!

In October 2008, my menstrual period ceased and this lasted for two years. I used several drugs and herbs, but to no avail.

When I told a colleague, who buys me Signs and Wonders Today publication about my predicament, she convinced me that my miracle was in this Church. She told me to stop using medications, and that once I come, my case would be settled. I believed her and that was how I joined this Commission in 2010.

That same month, I partook in the 21-day Prayer and Fasting. A day to the end of the fast, a lady shared her

testimony of how the God of David Oyedepo restored her menstrual period after two years. I keyed in to that testimony and **claimed my miracle with a heart of joy.** That same day, immediately I got home, my menstrual period was restored. I give God the glory!
–**Emmanuella, D.**

Divine Restoration via Unspeakable Joy!

Last year, I lost my job; so I decided to further my studies and I got two admissions from the United States of America (USA). Before I travelled, I got married, and we attended the Basic Certificate Course (BCC) and Leadership Certificate Course (LCC) of the Word of Faith Bible Institute (WOFBI).

There, our understanding broadened on what the Marriage Covenant was all about. So, I decided not to travel to the United States without my wife.

We were able to secure our visas, but when we got there, we were told that my wife's visa could not be changed from visitors' visa to students' visa. So, I deferred the admission until August. **That was how we left America with excitement.**

The following day, we arrived Nigeria and I started receiving messages that my former employer had been looking for me. I went there and they said, 'Please, we *want you back. On your resumption, we have a company house, an official car and other fringe benefits waiting for you.' I give God all the praise!* –**Akarakiri, F.**

Nine Years Barrenness Terminated!

*We got married in 2003 and since then, we believed God for the fruit of the womb. When we came to Canaanland to seek the face of God, we were privileged to see and be prayed for by Dr David Oyedepo; and he said that our desires were granted. **We returned joyful and continued to serve God** in the Winners' Satellite Fellowship (WSF).*

On the Liberation Night in May 2003, God blessed my family with a baby girl. Also, my brother in Spain had believed God for the fruit of the womb for 12 years. Last week Wednesday, God blessed him with a baby boy. I give God all the glory! –**Ikechukwu, S.**

20 Years Eye Problem Healed!

For 20 years, I had an eye problem. During one of the services, a lady testified of how she declared that she would not return to school with her glasses. That testimony hit me and I keyed in to it.

__While I was dancing and praising God__ for something different, a voice told me to drop my glasses where I was seated. I gained courage, left the glasses, took my Bible and started going home.

On my way to where I would board a bus, the voice told me again to go and testify about what God had done. I said, 'I have not checked myself; how do I testify?' He said, 'Go and testify!'

So, I returned to document my testimony with one of the pastors. In the process, I could see what he was writing clearly. Now, I can see and write without my glasses. Glory to God! –**Chinyem, C.**

26 Years Object In Ear Removed!

When I was a child, I used a pencil to clean my ear and it got stuck in it for 26 years. After taking the Communion during one of the Midweek Services, I put some in my ear.

I went to work that night and **while at work, I danced and praised God.** My colleagues stared at me and wondered why I was dancing. They asked if I had won anything and I said, 'No, there is something God is about to do for me tonight.'

At midnight, I felt something in my ear; I used an object to pull it out and I realised it was the pencil that had been in my ear for 26 years! Praise the Lord!"
–**Ikechukwu, S.**

10 Years Barrenness Destroyed!

We joined this Commission in July 2009 through a doctor friend, because we have been expecting a child for seven years.

During one of the services, Dr David Oyedepo said, 'If you have been coming to this Church for three months and nothing happens in your life, you better check yourself.' That day, I said, 'God, this is the place I want to be.' **I saw that there is joy here and I felt it inside me.**

During the Covenant Day of Fruitfulness in August, I came with my baby items for twins. I told God that I wanted a boy and a girl. I also came with my husband's picture, because one of the over 20 hospitals we visited diagnosed him with low sperm count, and I with hormonal imbalance.

Before I got home that day, my husband called me and said, 'It's settled.' That was how I became pregnant and delivered my baby to the glory of God. –**Mr. & Mrs. Ben, D.**

Encounter with Joy Articles!

I am one of Pastor (Mrs.) Faith Oyedepo's regular readers who enjoy the column, Family Matters, published in the Saturday Punch. I really enjoyed two of the published articles titled, No Food for the Idle Man and You Must Work.

I derived so much joy from those articles that I easily digested them, along with the words of wisdom that followed! –**Okwudiri, O.**

Supernatural Turnaround!

On January 2, 2014, when we resumed work, I was told to resign. I said that they came at a wrong time, because that was the season of prayer and fasting. When I returned from work, **I danced and told the God of my father to cause a turnaround.**

Thereafter, I wrote the names of all my bosses on a paper, placed it in a Communion bottle and locked them up. Lo and behold, when my boss returned from his trip abroad, I went to enquire from him and he said he didn't tell me to resign. He later asked me to work with him personally and thereafter, sent me to head the company he just bought abroad.

It pays to serve God because I'm a Zonal Minister and my wife is a chorister. We have served God and He has been faithful! –**Dennis, A.**

Career Breakthrough!

I lost my job in 2010; as a result, I experienced hardship. I joined this Commission in 2011, partook in the 21-day prayer and fasting, and attended the Word of Faith Bible

Institute (WOFBI) as well as Shiloh in December.

After the fast, I keyed in to the prophetic word from Dr David Oyedepo that undeniable, inexplicable and unfathomable testimonies would be my portion. **It became a song in my family.**

In 2012, I started a business and God gave us 'manna' to pay the bills. In February, I received a call from someone who said they got my Curriculum Vitae (CV) somewhere and they wanted me to restructure their company in Nigeria. Meanwhile, I had not submitted my CV to any company since 2010.

Each time I hear people share testimonies of N15million, N20million salaries, it baffled me. So, when asked about my salary offer, I said I wanted N15million. Miraculously, I was offered N18million.

While I was rejoicing over that, I received another call from a company, in Dubai, that they wanted me to start a business for them in Africa. To the glory of God, I was scheduled for training in Dubai the following weekend!
–Omoyele, K.

12 Years Marital Unrest Terminated!

I had been married for 12 years but I never enjoyed marital bliss. My family rejected me because I refused to file for a divorce.

When Dr David Oyedepo taught on the Ark Bearer's Sacrifice, during one of the services, I did not have anything to give because I had been jobless for a year. Then the Holy Spirit said, 'How about your wedding ring?'

With tears, I dropped the ring in an envelope and said, 'God, as I drop this ring, restore my marriage and give me a job.' **Immediately, I discovered that the depression I felt before had left! I was so happy!**

On getting home, I was ready for another confrontation with my husband. But to my amazement, he said, 'Honey welcome! How was church and your Bishop? You look tired. Go and take your bath, I have prepared food for you to eat.' I did not believe it; I thought it was a trick, so I went to the kitchen. Lo and behold, it was true!

When we finished eating, he noticed I was surprised, so he told me of his encounter. He said while I was in Church, he laid down to watch the television; suddenly, he heard an audible voice that called him and said, 'Sit up! What have you done about your marriage? Set your home aright.'

He said that made him go on his knees weeping, and he told God he was sorry. That day marked the beginning of good things in our marriage. I never knew that marriage could be so blissful! –**Agbetiku, U.**

As I conclude this chapter, I want you to take particular

note of this scripture:

I have taken your testimonies as a heritage forever,
For they are the joy of my heart.

Psalm 119:111 (WEB)

Without any doubt, I believe you have not only read but seen (through the eyes of your understanding) in practical terms, how the tool of joy can be used to provoke your turnaround in any unwanted situation.

God, Who is no respecter of persons (Acts 10:34-35) and cannot lie (Titus 1:2), is ready to replicate in your life what He did for those whose testimonies were recounted above.

As you put God in remembrance of His Word (Isaiah 43:26), and engage this powerful force of joy as a lifestyle, it is my prayer that every aspect of these undeniable acts of God that you desire shall be duplicated in your life, even in a greater dimension, in Jesus' name. Amen!

Salvation Prayer

The only condition God places before you to becoming His child is to accept Jesus Christ as your Lord and personal Saviour (**Romans 10:10**). Having considered this truth, you can now say this prayer:

Father, I realise that I have been a sinner. Today, I come before You asking for forgiveness of my sins. I believe in the death and resurrection of Jesus Christ and I believe in His power to save me if I ask Him to. Now Lord, save me, accept me as Your child and write my name in the book of life. Thank you Father for saving me, in Jesus' Name. I receive and accept You today as my Lord and personal Saviour. Amen.

Notes

ABOUT THE *Author*

Faith Abiola Oyedepo has, through the leading of the Holy Spirit, brought hope, joy and peace into many families and homes.

For many years since she received the ministry for families and homes, she has in no little measure dedicated her life to showing people the perfect will of God concerning their family relationships and homes. Her regular and scintillating weekly newspaper and internet columns - Family Matters, Family Success and Family Life, among others - have helped in no small measure in achieving this goal.

Also, she has a divine mandate to enrich the lives of singles and unmarried persons in a unique way.

She reaches out to the less privileged, the needy and those in the valley of decision, through her Faith Abiola Oyedepo Foundation (FAOF).

Pastor Faith has written over 20 anointed and impactful books that have transformed many lives and given them change of stories, including her best-selling title: *Rescued From Destruction*.

An anointed preacher of the Gospel, Pastor Faith has been doggedly supportive of her husband (Dr David O. Oyedepo, the Visionary/President Of Living Faith Church Worldwide Inc.) in the work of the ministry. They are parents to four children – David Jnr., Isaac, Love and Joys.

Books By Faith Oyedepo

- Guidelines To Effective Personal Bible Study
- Dating: A Biblical Guide
- The Force Of Joy
- The Force Of Hope
- Building A Successful Family
- Making Marriage Work
- Success In Marriage *(Co-authored with Dr David Oyedepo)*
- Marriage Covenant
- Raising Godly Children
- Rescued From Destruction
- Single With A Difference
- The Effective Minister's Wife
- The Spirit Of Faith
- A Living Witness *(Expanded version)*
- Nurturing The Incorruptible Seed *(Expanded version)*
- Service: The Master Key *(Expanded version)*
- The Dignity Of The Believer *(Expanded version)*
- Growing In Grace
- The Power Of The Communion Table
- Healing, Health And Wholeness
- Overcoming Anxiety
- Salvation: The Way Of Escape
- The Healing Scriptures
- The Healing Ministry Of Jesus Christ
- You Are Welcome To God's Family
- Understanding Motherhood

INSIDE VIEW OF
Faith Tabernacle

Dr David Oyedepo is the Founding President of the Living Faith Church Worldwide Inc. and the Senior Pastor of the Faith Tabernacle, a 50,000 capacity sanctuary located in Canaanland, Ota, a suburb of Lagos, Nigeria.

The construction of this gigantic architectural masterpiece was completed within twelve months and dedicated on September 18, 1999, built totally debt-free and without any foreign inputs! To God alone be all the glory.

Today, Faith Tabernacle stands as the home of signs and wonders for men and women all over the world, who keep coming in droves to worship the King of kings and the Lord of lords, Jesus Christ the Son of the Living God.

OUTSIDE VIEW OF FAITH TABERNACLE

OVERVIEW OF FAITH TABERNACLE

Visit our website for more information: www.faithtabernacle.org.ng

Covenant University

Centre For Research Innovation And Discovery (CUCRID)

Dr David Oyedepo is the Visioner and Chancellor of Covenant University, founded 21st October 2002. Today, Covenant University has a student population of over 6,000, all fully boarded on campus; in state of the art halls of residence. All degree programmes offered at Covenant University are fully accredited by the appropriate accrediting body. Presently, CU offers 42 degree programmes in 3 different faculties:

COLLEGE OF SCIENCE AND TECHNOLOGY:

Computer Science, Management Information System, Architecture, Building Technology, Estate Management, Industrial Mathematics, Industrial Chemistry, Industrial Physics, Biochemistry, Biology, Microbiology, Computer Engineering, Information and Communication Technology, Electrical and Electronic Engineering, Civil Engineering, Mechanical Engineering, Chemical Engineering, Petroleum Engineering.

COLLEGE OF HUMAN DEVELOPMENT:

Philosophy, Psychology, Counselling, English Language, Mass Communication, Public Relations and Advertising, Sociology and French.

COLLEGE OF BUSINESS AND SOCIAL SCIENCES:

Accounting, Taxation and Public Sector Accounting, Banking and Finance, Business Administration, Marketing, Industrial Relations and Human Resource Management, Economics, Demography and Social Statistics, International Relations, Political Science, Public Administration, Policy and Strategic Studies.

Visit our website for more information: **www.covenantuniversity.edu.ng**

Some Facilities at Covenant University

African Leadership Development Centre

4,000-Seat University Chapel

Post Graduate Halls Of Residence

Landmark University

Senate Building

Landmark University is a product of the education mandate given to Dr David Oyedepo, the President of the Living Faith Church Worldwide. Dedicated on the 21st of March 2011, it is the second university to be established by the church.

The vision of the University is to raise leaders with particular emphasis on promoting agricultural enterprise. The purpose of this focus of the University is to provide a learning platform that makes her graduates, leaders in meeting the food needs of the nation and solving the food security challenges of humanity.

The teaching, research and community services of the University are weaved around the intellectual and natural resource endowment of her immediate community.

Landmark University Offers the following courses:

COLLEGE OF AGRICULTURAL SCIENCES:

General Agriculture, Animal Science, Plant Science, Agricultural Extension & Rural Development, Agricultural Economics.

COLLEGE OF SCIENCE & ENGINEERING:

Industrial Chemistry, Industrial Mathematics, Industrial Physics, Computer Science, Biology, Biochemistry, Microbiology, Electrical And Information Engineering, Mechanical Engineering, Chemical Engineering, Civil Engineering, Agricultural Engineering.

COLLEGE OF BUSINESS & SOCIAL SCIENCES:

Accounting, Banking And Finance, Business Administration, Economics, Sociology, Political Science, International Relations.

Visit our website for more information: **www.lmu.edu.ng**

Some Facilities at Landmark University

University Library

University Chapel

Students' Hall Of Residence